THE

GREENS BOOK

PHOTOGRAPHY BY JOE COCA

SUSAN BELSINGER
& CAROLYN DILLE

INTERWEAVE PRESS

The Greens Book
Susan Belsinger and Carolyn Dille

Design, Susan Wasinger/Signorella Graphic Arts
Photography, Joe Coca except as follows: Susan Belsinger pages 44 and 45
Photo styling, Linda Ligon
Hand painted dishes, Dorrice Pyle
Production, Marc McCoy Owens

Interweave Press, Inc.
201 East Fourth Street
Loveland, Colorado 80537
USA

Printed in Hong Kong by Sing Cheong

Library of Congress Cataloging-in-Publication Data

Belsinger, Susan.
    The greens book / by Susan Belsinger and Carolyn Dille.
        p.   cm.
    Includes bibliographical references and index.
    ISBN 1-883010-05-5 : $14.95
    1. Cookery (Greens)   I. Dille, Carolyn.   II. Title.
TX803.G74B44   1994
641.6'54—dc20   94-38617
                                                        CIP

First Printing: 30M:1194:CC

This book is for our dear friend Tom DeBaggio, who has the greenest

thumb and heart of any gardener and writer we know.

His advice, encouragement, and gifts of plants and seeds

over the years have been invaluable and have fostered the confidence to

expand our growing horizons.

ACKNOWLEDGEMENTS

"Team work" and "group effort" may be buzz words in some quarters, but they describe a fine and tangible reality in making books with Interweave Press. Our thanks to the entire staff for understanding that collaboration can be harmonious and productive, and for their enthusiasm and support. Once again, our sincere appreciation and admiration to Linda Ligon, our editor and publisher, for her editing and styling skills, her ideas, and her dedication to our work. Thanks to Joe Coca for his artful and realistic photography and the spirit of fun and adventure in his studio that makes these books so handsome, as well as to his able assistant Lisa Rabold. We are also grateful for the editing skills of Judith Durant, the promotional and organizational talents of Barbara Ciletti and Gail Jones, and the special, graceful eye for design that Susan Wasinger brings to each of our books.

We are always glad of the opportunity to thank our friends and families for their abilities and willingness to taste-test, lend props, and babysit. Special thanks to Lucie and Cady for letting Susan get some work done. And to Deborah Hall for sharing in sowing, growing, and transplanting, to Sam Bettien for his gardening assistance, and to Kathleen Halloran for growing greens in Colorado for us. Last, but not least, we raise our glasses to Tomaso and Dick, the men who constantly love and support us, even when we immerse ourselves in new book projects.

THE GREENS BOOK

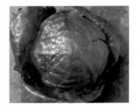

How many generations of mothers have encouraged/commanded their children, "Eat your greens; they're good for you"? And in how many languages have these ringing words been spoken? It's likely that the generations extend to prehistoric times, and the languages are many. The fact is that greens are tasty; why many children leave them until last on the plate is one of life's minor mysteries. Certainly, the flavors of many are complex, and cover a wide range: mild, sharp, sweet, tangy, delicate, bittersweet, even meaty. It seems we need experience and time to learn and appreciate these flavor relationships.

The greens to which our own mothers referred were chiefly spinach and cabbage. We don't remember needing much encouragement to eat spinach; we rather liked it, probably because we were served fresh cooked leaves, not canned or frozen. But Popeye was a popular cartoon character then, and we remember our mothers' drawing the point of how big and strong we could be. Spinach and olive oil became a favorite combination later. We weren't so keen on cabbage, except for coleslaw and corned beef and cabbage, only later appreciating its brassy flavor and learning how to cook it well. We liked salad, usually iceberg lettuce, dressed up on occasion with tomatoes or shredded carrots, or mayonnaise rather than oil and vinegar. Of all the vegetables, we liked tomatoes, corn, and carrots from the farm produce stands best, as much for the adventure of going out to the country as for their just-picked flavor. It has been our adventures as cooks and gardeners, however, that have given us such wide regard for greens and other vegetables, and for their flavors, histories, beauty, dependability, and plain goodness.

Delectable Tom Thumb, a butterhead lettuce (Lactuca sativa), fresh from the garden.

Our knowledge of greens is worlds away from what we knew twenty and thirty years ago. It's no longer true that "*. . . garden lettuce with leafy head/ Is hard to get as unsliced bread*", as the immortal Ogden Nash once complained. Garden lettuce, sometimes as fine as the English herbalists Evelyn, Gerard, and Culpepper raved about several centuries ago, is now available in restaurants, supermarkets, farmers' markets, and urban, suburban, and country gardens across the nation. And not only lettuce, but all manner of greens, from radicchio to mizuna, flowering Italian mustard to flowering Chinese mustard. Even five years ago, most of these greens were not grown on a commercial scale, nor offered in many seed catalogs.

A confluence of factors is swelling this rediscovery of greens: interest in eating healthy foods, fueled by medical research into many foodstuffs; an influx of immigrant populations who brought their favorite greens with them; the ease of growing most greens, even in small spaces; and the desire for plate and palate novelty shown by many food professionals. Far from being new, the greens that we consider in this book have been eaten from earliest history, and undoubtedly before. As food fashions wax and wane, some have become popular, some have fallen from favor, and some have been improved by agricultural techniques.

In this book, we define greens as succulent leaves and stems eaten cooked or raw. They include herbs, flowers, and vegetables, annuals and perennials, and their colors range from pale jade green, deep forest green, and brilliant yellow-green to fuchsia and magenta. Greens represent many different plant families and they come from cultures around the world.

This grab-bag definition of greens has long been customary in Anglo-American countries, perhaps because greens are naturally abundant and generally easy to grow. Celery fits the greens description, but is never so classified. It takes more work to grow than lettuce or cabbage, but then so do blanched Belgian endive and radicchio, which are usually called greens, even though their colors are often not green.

A common definition of greens limits the selection to the conventionally green kale, collards, mustard, turnip, spinach, chard, and beet greens. Lettuces are included, usually with the modifier "salad". However, choosing from a more expansive group of greens offers a wealth of pleasurable eating and growing experiences, as we will show.

LOCAL AND GLOBAL GREENS

Greens are grown and eaten the world over, and there is a vast number of types and varieties. Every ethnic cuisine has its favorites, and has evolved particular ways to eat and cook them. Cabbage is so important to the Chinese that the word for cabbage and vegetable is the same: *choi*. In Dutch and Italian *groente* and *verdure* are words for the color green, as well as referring to vegetable produce in general.

In the United States, Native Americans eat lamb's-quarters. Alaskans and Canadians grow 60-pound cabbages, for which they have to think of many dishes. Some Midwesterners stew amaranth like spinach. New Englanders always include cabbage in their boiled dinner. Southerners eat collard, turnip, and mustard greens, usually with a bit of ham or bacon. Most Americans make

Red Stripe leaf amaranth (Amaranthus tricolor), left, and New Zealand spinach (Tetragonia tetragonioides) are good in salads when the leaves are about this size, 1 to 3 inches long.

iceberg lettuce salads and believe that the dandelion is their enemy. Because California is home to people from many regions of the U.S. and the world, Californians eat all of the above and most greens below.

The Chinese have tat sois and pak chois from the cabbage family to stir-fry, and heading cabbage, such as Napa, to pickle. The Dutch use cabbages for salads (coleslaw comes from the Dutch *kool*, "cabbage" and *sla*, "salad"), as well as endive and kale for stamppot, mashed potatoes with greens. The Japanese have perilla for sushi, and mizuna for soups and salads. The Irish have cabbages to make colcannon, a favorite national dish of potatoes and cabbage. The French use mâche, frisée, and sorrel in salads, soups, and sauces. The English serve steamed sea kale with butter and lemon juice, and make a mess of spring greens with Good-King-Henry of the chenopodium family, among others. Lamb's-quarters and epazote, members of the same family, and purslane are cooked with chiles in Mexico. Italians are great greens lovers, counting as their favorites various lettuces, arugula, and misticanza for salads, and spinach and chard for cooking in many ways. Australians and New Zealanders prepare New Zealand spinach, unrelated to common spinach, with European and Oriental seasonings.

Greens, like other plants that humans have depended on for a long time, are well represented in the historical record. The Egyptians recorded lettuce growing around 4500 B.C., and painted Cos (Romaine-type) lettuces in the tombs of royalty. The Sumerians listed cress, lettuce, mustard, and turnips among the crops they grew in 2500 B.C. The ancient Greeks and Romans greatly fancied greens, particularly lettuces. The Romans ate stem lettuce (celtuce), Cos lettuce, endive, chicory, and mallow in salads. One rather elaborate Roman recipe for a mixed green salad dressing contains fresh soft cheese, honey, wine, fish sauce, vinegar, herbs, pine nuts, dates, and raisins. Though the ancients had not codified vitamin and mineral contents, they knew which greens to gather and to cultivate for nutrition and flavor, and which to celebrate with stories and recipes.

The Cook's Garden offers a variety of Italian cutting chicories, such as this Biondissima Trieste (Cichorium intybus).

Egyptian, Greek, and Roman legends and myths about lettuce center on its supposed procreative, amatory, and erotic properties. Goddesses and gods mate with lettuce, turn one another into lettuce, and feed it to one another for purpose of seduction. They sleep on beds of lettuce as well; its reputation as a soothing, sleep-inducing plant has been remarkably consistent up until the last century. Aristoxenus, a Greek philosopher and musicologist of the fourth century B.C., gave one of the nicest ancient recipes for preparing lettuce: he sprinkled his lettuces in the evening with wine and honey, picked them at dawn the next day, and called them green cakes given to him by the earth.

The Jewish ritual of eating sorrel and other bitter herbs at Passover is thousands of years old, and many Jewish people continue to eat bitter and other greens as part of their everyday diet. This tradition influenced the use by some Christians of bitter greens and herbs at Easter. An Easter soup of watercress, sorrel, dandelion, chervil, and spinach is still made in Bavaria. Spinach came to Europe from Persia and the Middle East during the Middle Ages, but it was probably cultivated much earlier farther to the East. The King of Nepal sent spinach plants to the Chinese rulers of the T'ang dynasty in the seventh century A.D., calling it a vinegar leaf vegetable, which describes the way many people serve it today: with vinegar or lemon juice.

Spinach is celebrated every September during the Spinach Festival in Lenexa, Kansas. Lenexa was settled by a large number of Belgian families, who cultivated spinach so well that it was the self-styled "Spinach Capital of the World" in the 1930s. The festival takes place in a city park, with an exhibit of Belgian artifacts and a spinach recipe contest, and it boasts the world's largest

spinach salad. Of course, the guest of honor is Popeye, who with Olive Oyl and the townspeople helps serve the salad.

Residents of Gaston, South Carolina, host an annual Collards Festival in October, serving up the greens with "a little bit of grease and a lot of love". 1994 marked the 12th festival; the event was started by a local farm woman, whose son, Walter Hook, donates the collards in her memory. In addition to a parade, Miss and Ms. Collard are crowned, collard cakes or other tidbits are passed around, and recipes such as collard kraut ("better than sauerkraut") are distributed. Miss Dot's traditional recipe for collard greens calls for removing the stems, blanching the leaves, and cooking them with a little water, bacon grease, and salt. These are served with vinegared hot pepper sauce and corn bread.

GOOD AND GOOD FOR YOU

You may forget the happy circumstance that greens are good for you; if you eat them, they will nourish you with abundant vitamins and minerals.

Even loose-leaf and butterhead lettuces, though lacking substantial amounts of the currently glamorous beta-carotene, contain goodly amounts of iron and vitamin A, as well as fiber. Variety, to us, is not just the spice of life, but the essence. Any particular green may have more or less of any particular vitamin, but by eating different greens you will add to the pleasures of your table and fulfill your body's needs at the same time.

Beta-carotene and related carotenoids, and vitamins B2 (riboflavin), C, and E are antioxidants: they prevent breakdown of complex chemicals in biological tissues and systems. These antioxidants are found in abundance in all the dark green greens—spinach, chard, collards, kale, beet, turnip, and mustard greens—and in red and yellow vegetables. Researchers are discovering that antioxidants seem to play a role in reducing breast cancer, heart disease, and cataracts. While we aren't ringing the latest miracle food bell, it certainly seems sensible and fun to eat a lot of greens.

Escarole (Cichorium endivia) is a broad-leaved chicory that is good raw in salads or cooked.

In the 1920s and '30s, vitamin and mineral contents were established for many unprocessed foods, including greens. They confirmed what people had known for centuries: greens are high in many elements necessary for good health. Calcium is found in kale, bok choi, dandelion and mustard greens, and watercress. Substantial amounts of iron are present in sorrel and endive, as well as the lettuces mentioned above. Chicories such as radicchio, Belgian endive, and escarole, as well as sorrel and loose-leaf lettuces are good sources of vitamin A. Sorrel also has a good amount of vitamins B2 and C. All the chicories contain significant vitamin C. Spinach, dandelion greens, mustard greens, and the cresses are at or near the top of practically every list: iron, calcium, phosphorus, potassium, vitamins A, B1, B2, niacin, and C. Spinach is also high in magnesium. Cabbages are related to mustards, and they contain the same vitamins and minerals, though usually in lesser amounts. Many supermarkets list at least some of these for common vegetables, along with calories and sodium. Because most greens contain sodium and other mineral salts, they need little, if any, added salt.

Wanting to get onto the goodness of greens on the plate, we will not go into detail about the lesser-known vitamin K, or the theories of how dandelion and mustard greens, spinach or kale can stimulate your sex life, make your hair shine and skin glow, or increase your mental acuity. We will say that greens have served us well, at our tables and in our gardens, and that we attribute at least some of our well-being to them, as many have done before us.

The Brassicas: Cabbages, Kales, Mustards, and Others

This very large group of greens belongs to the mustard family. It includes smooth and savoy cabbage, Oriental cabbages, kale, collards, mustards, mizuna, and turnip greens. Head cabbages (*Brassica oleracea*, Capitata group) can be round, cone-shaped, or flat-headed. The smooth-leafed cabbages come in pale green, medium green, or red. The crinkle-leafed savoy has dark green outer leaves and a medium green-yellow heart. Some varieties that we have liked are Golden Acre, Market Prize, Blue Ribbon, Grand Slam, Savoy King, and Dutch Savoy Baby Promoso. Heading Chinese cabbages (*B. rapa*, Pekinensis group) are cylindrical or barrel-shaped. Napa or Celery, Michihli, and Jade Pagoda are good varieties to try. Non-heading Chinese cabbages (*B. rapa*, Chinensis group) include the attractive and delicious bok or pak choi, and tat soi, a rosette form of pak choi.

Kale (*B. oleracea*, Acephala group) includes ornamental greens that add vivid colors to the fall and winter garden, and to plates as garnishes, but are not notably tasty, though tender center leaves can be eaten. Kale is thought to be the ancestor of all cabbages; its blue-green leaves are not only decorative in the garden, but garden kale is much tastier than what the supermarket offers. Ragged Jack, also called Red Russian, and Dwarf Curly Blue are particular favorites of ours. Collards in the same group look very much like smooth-leafed kale, though they are more green than blue, and taste a little milder than many kinds of kale.

The flowering mustards (*B. rapa*) include the delicious broccoli di rabe (*B. r.*, Ruvo Group) with white flowers. Some of its close relatives have yellow flowers; common and market names are used rather loosely: cima di rapa, broccoletto, broccoli raab or rape, galluzzi, and gallizi. Pak choi (*B. r.*, Chinensis Group) is harvested at several stages, including when its white flowers form. Choi sum (*B. parachinensis*) is usually harvested when buds and flowers have formed. It comes in yellow- and purple-flowered varieties.

Mustard greens (*B. juncea*) are usually tangy, even peppery in flavor, and are excellent winter greens, being hardy and having the best flavor in very cool weather. The smooth-leafed types, which may be called India, China, or brown mustard, are usually stronger tasting than the curly types. They are commonly bright yellow-green, though some, such as Red Giant and Osaka Purple, are

The color of red cabbage (Brassica oleracea, Capitata Group) and its slightly tangy flavor make it especially good in salads.

medium-green with red or purple coloration.

Mizuna (*B. r.*, Japonica Group), a favorite soup green in Japan, has become a popular salad green in large urban areas in the United States. It has decorative, cut leaves and a mild flavor. Finest texture and color come from cool weather sowings, though it can also be grown in summer. If leaves become tough during hot weather, harvest them for cooked greens; their bland taste tames the flavor of strong greens.

Turnip greens (*B. rapa*, Rapifera Group) can be harvested by cutting the young tender greens from turnips before they become rough. The greens are quite peppery, but combine well with milder ones. Tyfon, a variety grown for greens, does not form root balls. The greens are smooth and mild when young and should be grown in cool weather. Other non-rooting cultivars grown for their tops are Just Right and All Top.

Spinach mustard (*B. rapa*, Perviridis Group) is a green deserving of more cultivation, as it is quick to mature (30 to 45 days), pleasant-tasting, and cut-and-come-again. Its unusual flavor combines mild cabbage, mustard, and spinach. Baby greens are a good salad accent; larger and summer-grown ones make a nice mess of greens. We like Tah Tsai, Tendergreen, and Komatsuna.

The Chicories: Endives, Escaroles, and Radicchios

Endive and escarole belong to one of the two main species of chicory grown for greens, *Cichorium endivia*. Endive, also called curly endive, is sometimes referred to as frisée when it is young. Escarole has broad, smooth leaves that distinguish it from endive, which has sharply cut and curled leaves. Both have the nutty bittersweet characteristic of the chicories, and both can be blanched in the garden to bring out their sweetness. We usually don't bother to blanch and have had success with very early spring and late summer/early autumn sowings of Galia, Très Fine Frisée, and Fine Maraîchère curly endives, and many escaroles, including Broad-leaved Batavian, Batavian Full Heart, and Sinco.

Belgian endive, also called witloof, and radicchios of all colors belong to the other chicory species grown for its greens, *C. intybus*. Belgian endive must be forced in a cool (about 50°F), dark environment to produce the tight, point-

Facing page, blanched Treviso (top) and Castelfranco radicchios (Cichorium intybus) have a nutty, bittersweet flavor.

Above, this unruly head of frisée is a small-leaved form of Cichorium endivia that is excellent in salads.

ed, pale yellow-green or rose-colored heads that command a high price in the market. The procedure was discovered by a Belgian farmer about 1875; he had thrown some wild chicory roots on a manure or compost pile during the fall. Several weeks later, he noticed the pale heads (called chicons) peeking through the compost. He cleaned and ate them, and found them to be delicious. We have not grown witloof, but varieties are now available that are said not to require soil for forcing.

Radicchios have been cultivated for centuries on the Italian peninsula and were as highly prized by the ancient Romans as they are by present-day Italians. Verona (the ball-headed red and white type found in American markets), Castelfranco, and Treviso cultivars are planted in early spring, and are cut back and blanched in the garden with the onset of cool weather. Their exceptional flavor and beauty make this a labor of love for us, but nonblanching types have been developed, of which we've enjoyed Rossana, Giulio, and the Sugarloaf varieties. The Sugarloaf types are green rather than red, and stay relatively sweet for leaf harvests throughout most summers, as long as they have plenty of water. All chicories are excellent in salads and in cooked dishes.

Cutting chicories are an intermediate form in which leaves are harvested when they are 3 to 6 inches tall. We especially like Biondissima Trieste and Spadona. They are worth cultivating as they are rare in North American markets.

Charlotte is a cultivar of Swiss chard (Beta vulgaris, Cicla Group) with red stems and veining.

Spinaches, Chards, and Beet Greens

Spinach (*Spinacia oleracea*) ranks just after lettuce as the most popular green in North America. It has gotten very good press for its nutrients for many years, and cooked or raw is very versatile in the kitchen, harmonizing with many other foods. Much work has been done to extend its growing season and resistance to diseases. Though we have tried many spinaches, the ones we like best are cool-weather varieties, especially the smooth-leafed European ones. Our favorites are Wolter, Nordic, Melody, Bloomsdale Long Standing, and Giant Nobel. New Zealand spinach (*Tetragonia tetragonioides*) belongs to a different family but is a good summer substitute for common spinach, as it is heat tolerant. It is close enough in flavor to work well in most cooked spinach dishes.

Red and golden beets belong to the Crassa Group of Beta vulgaris.

Chard (*Beta vulgaris, ssp. cicla*) and beet greens (*B. vulgaris, ssp. crassa*) are closely related; chard has been cultivated for several centuries as a leaf crop only; it does not form swollen roots. Chard (also called Swiss chard or perpetual spinach) is a prolific and reliable performer in most gardens, and surpasses beets in yielding good-flavored greens even during the hottest months, provided that it has plenty of water. Both red and green varieties are tasty; we like the red for its beautiful color and slightly more mineral flavor, and the green for its meaty, thick white stalks and mellow flavor. Ruby Red, Rhubarb, Charlotte, Paros, and Erbette are varieties that we have become fond of.

Thinning the beet row is one of the special edible pleasures we have as gardeners, undoubtedly because we love beet greens so much. Beets do not grow well, or at all, in hot weather, and should thus be planted as early as possible in spring, then again in late summer or early autumn. All beet greens are edible; we like Detroit Dark Red and Lutz Salad Leaf.

Yellow or golden orach (Atriplex hortensis), also called mountain spinach, may be prepared just like other spinach. It is a little milder in flavor.

Lettuces: Heads and Loose-leaves

The four main kinds of lettuce (*Lactuca sativa*) are classified by shape and growth habit, regardless of leaf color. Cos or Romaine types are upright and cylindrical, and take longer to mature than butterhead and leaf lettuces. There are red-edged, pale golden green, and deep green varieties. We like the venerable Cos, as well as Jericho, Paris White, Valmaine, Diamond Gem (a miniature for hearts of romaine), and Rouge d'Hiver for red romaine. Cos lettuces are one of the two oldest lettuces, and are named for the Greek island of Kos. They and the loose-leaf lettuces have almost double the vitamins and minerals of other kinds.

Lolla Rossa red leaf lettuce (Lactuca sativa) adds color and texture to salads.

Loose-leaf lettuces are the easiest lettuces to grow and the most popular with home gardeners. The group offers many beautiful shades of coloration, and the plants mature quickly, in about 45 to 60 days. They can be harvested over a long period by cutting or snapping outer leaves, or by taking entire heads. We have experimented with many varieties and recommend the following ones highly: Salad Bowl, Black-Seeded Simpson, Red Sails, Green or Red Oak Leaf, Red Deer Tongue, Pirat, and Biondo Lisce.

Crisphead lettuces include most of the lettuce commercially grown in North America, notably iceberg. These types take 75 to 100 days to mature and do best in cool weather. We have grown and enjoyed Great Lakes, Red Grenoble, and Green Ice.

Butterhead lettuces, a subdivision of crispheads, are characterized by their tender leaves softly folded in loose rosettes. Heads grow close to the ground and are usually rather small. Boston, Bibb, Butterhead, Brune d'Hiver (an over-wintering type), Italian Perella Red, and Tom Thumb (a miniature) are good varieties, and Four Seasons is outstanding, with its lovely red and green outer leaves and pink and pale yellow inner ones.

Celtuce (*L. s.*, Angustana Group) is thought to be the oldest cultivated lettuce. It is called stem or asparagus lettuce, as the stem is the part that is eaten and it tastes slightly of asparagus. It is a large plant, about the size of heading cabbages, and takes about three months to mature. We have not grown it; seed is not common here, though it is still cultivated extensively in China.

Sorrel (Rumex acetosa) has a lemon-sour flavor and is good cooked or raw.

Herb Greens: Rocket, Cresses, Sorrel, and Perilla

Rocket (*Eruca vesicaria ssp. sativa*) is an ancient plant, cultivated or gathered from the wild in most Mediterranean countries; it has recently become popular in North America. Its several Italian names indicate how widespread it is on that peninsula: arugula, ruchetta, rucola. Rocket's distinctive taste is peppery and nutty and has been described as smoky, or like mustard, peanuts, radish, horseradish, and bacon. The flavors become muted when rocket is cooked, but it still has a richness and depth unlike any other green. The cream-colored, purple-veined small flowers make excellent garnishes.

The cresses belong to different genera within the mustard family and have different cultivation requirements but all have a peppery flavor. Watercress (*Nasturtium officinale*) flourishes near streams or running water. It is the most nutritious of all the cresses. Upland or winter cress (*Barbarea verna*) is a cool season biennial, generally winter hardy, with the same growing requirements as watercress. It is grown commercially to extend the cress season. The leaves distinguish it from true watercress; they are larger, longer, and pointed, though the same deep green. *B. verna* should not be confused with *B. bulgaris* in the wild; the latter is not edible. Garden cress (*Lepidium sativum*) can be grown as sprouts or in the garden for its greens. It is also called peppergrass and curly cress; there are several flat-leafed cultivars.

Sorrel, a perennial plant rich in vitamins and minerals, belongs to the buckwheat family. Two species are commonly cultivated. French sorrel (*Rumex scutatus*) has arrow-shaped leaves and is somewhat less acidic than common sorrel (*R. acetosa*). Its lemony-tart flavor is a good accent in salads and with other cooked greens.

Perilla (*Perilla frutescens*), a member of the mint family, is a popular Oriental potherb, called *shiso* in Japan, where it is also used in sushi. Tender young leaves add a rather perfumey, pleasant taste to mixed green salads, and whole plants can be harvested to stew with other greens, or alone. All the perillas we've grown—green, Purple, and Cumin-scented—are rather ornamental plants with bushy growth and frilled leaves. The purple variety looks very much like ruffled Opal basil.

Salad Mixes: Mesclun, Misticanza, and Others

Salad mixes have become popular in North American during the past few years. In supermarkets, they are usually called spring mix, baby lettuce mix, or baby greens mix. These mixes are based on the tradition carried on in Europe for centuries of gathering young, wild greens from the fields for salads. At some time people began to cultivate similar greens in their gardens. The French and Italians have by now codified these cultivated mixtures according to their tastes. Both *mesclun* (French) and *misticanza* (Italian) mean "mixture". They contain lettuces, usually loose-leaf and both green and red, chicories of several kinds, often arugula and/or garden cress, corn salad, as well as dandelion and chervil. The plants are chosen for their cut-and-come-again qualities. *The Cook's Garden Catalog* (see page 109), has developed a variety of mixes for different growing situations and tastes.

Home-Grown Greens: Amaranth, Chrysanthemum, Corn Salad, Dandelion, Good-King-Henry, Lamb's-quarters, Orach, and Others

The greens we consider in this section are ones we seldom see, or have never seen in U. S. markets, though most are cultivated for sale in other parts of the world. Many grow wild here, are easy in the garden, and interesting in the kitchen.

Amaranth (*Amaranthus tricolor* and *cvs.*) is an ancient annual plant grown throughout the world for greens, grain, and flowers. It is also called Chinese spinach and tampala. The leaves are quite tasty cooked and can substitute for spinach during the summer. Choose varieties developed especially for greens, such as Greek, Hijau Salad, and Coleus Leaf Salad, offered in the *Seeds of Change Catalog* (see page 109).

Garland chrysanthemum (*Chrysanthemum coronarium*) is usually sold as the common small yellow-flowered bedding plant, rather than for its greens. Occasionally we find it in Oriental farmers' stalls at farmers' markets. They sell it in bunches in the spring, as many Oriental peoples consider it a spring tonic green and diuretic. It has a pungent yet refreshing slight tartness. We like it uncooked in mixed green salads, and steamed very lightly, just enough to wilt, as well as stir-fried.

Corn salad (*Valerianella locusta*) is much prized as a salad delicacy in Northern Europe, England, and France, where it is also called lamb's lettuce and mâche. We will not be surprised when it begins to appear here. Its flavor is mild but full, its texture tender yet toothsome. It goes well with a great many salad ingredients and dressings. In addition, it is lovely, with small spoon-shaped leaves that grow in rosettes in most varieties. We have tried many— Cavallo, Broadleaved, Verte de Cambrai, Grosse Graine Dutch, Piedmont,

Opposite:
Goldgelber purs-
lane, top, is tart
and lemony-
tasting, while
amaranth is mild
and colorful.

Dandelion greens (Taraxacum officinale) may be harvested from your yard or garden for a home forager's treat. They have the best flavor in winter and early spring when the leaves are 3 to 6 inches long.

and Coquille—and like them all for their slightly different flavors, textures, and shapes.

Although we know that dandelion (*Taraxacum officinale*) is usually considered a weed in the United States, to be extirpated with unpronounceable chemicals, it was not always that way, and it is still a well-respected pot and salad green in many quarters. It is very nutritious, and needs only to be respected in the garden and kitchen to be very tasty. We have picked 3- to 4-inch-long leaves from the wild dandelion in our grass, and they were pretty good, but the best flavor, and broader leaves, are found in the cultivated French strains, of which we have grown Montmagny.

Of the several cultivated members of the Chenopodium family, Good-

King-Henry (*Chenopodium bonus-henricus*) and lamb's-quarters (*C. album*) are grown for their use as cooked greens. We find them a bit metallic-tasting when raw, no doubt because of their high mineral content. Other people think they taste like spinach and are delicious in salads, while still others call them bland. Magenta Spreen lamb's-quarters is a handsome variety, with green and fuchsia-pink coloration.

Orach (*Atriplex hortensis*), also called mountain spinach, is one of our favorite uncommon greens. Its flavor is more similar to spinach than most other spinach substitutes, if a little milder. The young plants offer very tasty salad leaves, and mature leaves are excellent cooked. We have tried green and yellow varieties, but Ruby is a star. Its stunning iridescent fuchsia and pale green leaves glow in the garden and in our salad bowls spring and fall.

To discuss all the greens cultivated around the world would fill a two-volume encyclopedia. There are many tropical greens that will not grow in temperate climates and mountain greens specific to certain regions, as well as what we term accent greens: those added in moderation to give a different interest to ordinary dishes. We like Goldgelber purslane (*Portulaca oleracea*, 'Goldgelber') for its special tartness, and mallow (*Malva verticillata*) for its decorative leaves. If you have the space and are an adventurous cook/gardener, you might try sea kale (*Crambe maritima*), which needs a permanent bed as asparagus does, and is said to taste like it. If you have a wooded area in your garden, you could plant miner's lettuce (*Montia perfoliata*), a pretty, mild, and tasty salad plant. Erbastella (*Plantago lanceolata*), also called barbe di prete, minutina, ripple grass, and buckhorn plantain is a salad green that we grew in Italy; its flavor is mild, but its 1/8-inch-wide, dark green crinkled leaves add visual interest to many salads.

Freshness and Flavor

For superior flavor and nutrition, pay particular attention to harvesting or choosing greens. Color is a good indicator of healthy greens. Kale should be a deep matte blue-green. Cabbages may be pale green to pale yellow-green, medium green, or red-purple, but the heads should be tightly closed. Common cabbage should be glossy, and heavy. Savoy and Napa types have a matte finish. Most greens should not show any yellow. Yellow-green types, such as Belgian endive and curly mustard should not show any brown. Lettuces and other salad greens have a great range of colors, but those that have been well grown and properly stored do not have brown spots or stems. At the market, look for spinach leaves that are a slightly glossy deep green, and still attached to their roots. Cutting greens exposes them to oxidation, which robs them of flavor and nutrients. White-stemmed chard from the market often is gray where the stems were cut and under the twist-ties if they have been bunched too tightly. This discoloration does not affect the flavor beyond the immediate area; trim it off with a stainless steel knife and use the chard within a day or two.

A fresh assortment of garden lettuces.

Greens are quite perishable. Those bought at supermarkets have already been stored a week or longer; using them on the day of purchase or the day after maximizes nutrition and flavor. Most greens can be stored in plastic bags in the vegetable crisper of the refrigerator. Watercress yellows very quickly; trim the stems and store them upright in a container with about an inch of water, covered with a plastic bag to prevent cold dehydration in the refrigerator.

In general, the thicker the leaves and the tighter the head, the longer greens can be stored under refrigeration. Head cabbages keep best, though even they will mold eventually. Kale, collards, savoy and Oriental cabbages, including pak choi, keep three or four days. Chard, spinach, turnip, mustard, and beet greens keep two or three days. Salad greens are the most perishable and may pick up a "refrigerator" flavor. Remove any brown or decaying bits from salad mixes, then wash, dry, and store them in plastic bags or a salad spinner for a day or so if you can't use them immediately.

Greens from farmers' markets and from our own gardens keep well on the rare occasions when we do not harvest them for immediate consumption, but because flavor is so important to the enjoyment of food, we prefer to eat our

greens as soon as possible. Even the strong-tasting greens—cabbages, mustard and turnip greens—appeal to people who profess not to like them when they are served fresh from the garden. As greens are composed chiefly of water, they present our palates with the elemental mineral flavors of earth and water, refined but distinct. Storage slowly dehydrates them and destroys the more subtle flavor compounds.

If you grow your own greens, you will find that you cannot always harvest for best flavor, when leaves are young, or plants are at the peak of maturity. In cool weather, greens will keep well on the plants. In the heat, they can become tough and/or bitter very quickly. We taste them to decide how to deal with less than ideal greens. When pot greens are past their prime, we blanch them, cook them a little longer, and season them strongly. When lettuces are a little old, with milky sap, we wash them well in vinegar water and trim the lower stems.

Dwarf Blue curly-leaf kale (Brassica oleracea, Acephala Group) is cold-hardy, attractive, and tasty.

Cooked Greens and Pot Likker

Now that you have some bunches of fresh, tasty greens, what will you do with them? This is the juncture, many people have told us, at which they "cannot think of anything different." There are thousands of ways to prepare greens; we usually choose simple ones, the better to relish the flavor and in the interest of time. Fortunately, it is no longer the fashion to boil greens to sogginess, then cover them with cream sauce or souse them in vinegar and grease. On the other hand, it is not always necessary simply to steam spinach or stir-fry mixed greens with soy sauce. Good as these dishes can be, we have noticed a resistance, even among those nearest and dearest to us, to the plain green. The currents of food preferences run deep; perhaps our affluent culture disdains greens as the wealthy did in previous times. Greens have always been abundant, inexpensive, and common. Some quirk in human nature seems to crave the exotic, luxurious, and rare, no matter how intrinsically good the common may be.

The first step is to wash greens well. The following technique does away with several washings to remove sand, grit, and critters. According to the amount of greens you have, fill the sink one-third to one-half full of cold water, or use a bowl or salad spinner. According to how much water you are using, add one tablespoon to one-quarter cup of vinegar to the water and stir it in a bit. Place trimmed greens in the vinegared water and swish them around. Let them stand for five to ten minutes or longer if you are busy doing other things.

Lift the greens from the water with a little care not to disturb the water. Greens washed with this method need only one wash about 90 percent of the time. If greens are caked with silt, rinse them well first under running water before putting them in the vinegar bath. The vinegar dislodges both soil particles and insects, which drop to the bottom of the container. The vinegar does not flavor the greens. Any vinegar can be used; we use ordinary distilled vinegar, as it is much less expensive than other kinds.

Red Russian kale (Brassica oleracea, Acephala Group), also called Ragged Jack, is beautiful and dependable in the garden, and delicious as well.

Now, cook up a mess of greens. We find that many strong-flavored greens benefit from a brief blanching, a minute to three or four, if they are served as a vegetable dish or with pasta. Kale, mustard and turnip greens, broccoli di rabe, and dandelion greens, when we are not using very young ones for salad, are greens that we usually blanch. Since many nutrients are water-soluble, we follow the Italian custom of cooking the pasta in the blanching water; the pasta absorbs some flavor as well. When we are not using the greens with pasta, we blanch in a small amount of water and save it for soups. Pot likker is a term used in the Southern U.S. for the rich broth that results from cooking a large amount of greens with a little water and seasonings. Corn bread is the traditional accompaniment to soak up the juices. One of our favorite cocktails is made by cooking spinach or chard in the water that clings to their leaves. If we are cooking them for further preparation, we drain the greens and pour the juice into a glass to drink while we are cooking.

Greens can be added to many dishes without making them the focal point. Hearty stews and soups are enlivened by chard and kale. Even more elegant pureed soups, made with carrot, potato, or tomato can be garnished with shredded colorful lettuces. Pasta dishes, especially rich meaty and/or creamy ones are brightened by strands of lettuce, rolled and cut like fettuccine, or by shreds of rocket. Pasta with fish is good with a few shreds of sorrel. Tat soi leaves or mizuna make even a simple miso broth soup look and taste special. Likewise, shredded spinach, sorrel, rocket, or lettuce works well with chicken broth. For the brightest flavor, pour the hot broth over the greens and serve immediately.

Potatoes combine especially well with greens. Try scalloped potatoes with chard, or leftover mashed potatoes mixed with shredded spinach and sautéed in patties, or potato and leek soup with sorrel. Potato salads are good garnished liberally with herb or tender greens, according to the flavors in the salads. We like to add shredded mizuna, spinach, sorrel, rocket, or garden cress to steamed rice when we fluff it. The rice looks pretty, and can accompany any number

Top, early summer unblanched garden radicchios, Castel-franco and Rossana, and bottom, Verona radicchio from the market, cultivars of Cichorium intybus.

of dishes, depending on the green chosen.

Greens are a wonderful addition to bread or corn bread stuffings, and are excellent in chicken or turkey stuffing that is placed under the skin. To make an-under-the skin stuffing, mix wilted and cooled spinach or chard with soft bread crumbs and perhaps ricotta cheese, and season well with nutmeg, pepper, chives or garlic chives, and onions or garlic.

Chicken, fish, ham, pork, sausage, and lamb go well with greens in stews, stuffings, or served on the side. Cabbage is eaten with ham and pork around the world, red cabbage in wine (the wine keeps the cabbage from turning blue) with pork chops, cutlets, or roast, and the many cabbage soups flavored with pork of some kind, including bacon. Kale, linguiça sausage, and potatoes are combined in a classic Portuguese soup-stew. When cabbage has some acid— wine, lemon, or vinegar—added to it, or is made into sauerkraut, it is served with duck and geese as well. Ground pork, lamb, or beef are mixed with cabbage to make the stuffed cabbage leaves of many European cuisines, pot stickers and other dumplings from the Orient, and the Russian piroshky—small flaky pastry pies. The English have many cabbage and beef dishes, including bubble and squeak: shredded blanched cabbage sautéed in butter with leftover roast beef, served with gravy or a tangy vinegar sauce.

The French, Italians, Portuguese, and Spanish like greens with legumes, especially white beans and chick peas. The many meatless soups from the Mediterranean usually contain onions, carrots, and herbs along with greens and legumes. A cooked salad that we like from the region is chick pea and blanched chard, with slivers of mild onion, dressed simply with olive oil and lemon juice or wine vinegar. We are also partial to white bean salads with different greens: raw or grilled radicchio, rocket; blanched chard. For a Middle Eastern/North African flavor, combine lentils with chard, kale, spinach, or cabbage and flavor with cumin, garlic, lemon, and a touch of hot peppers. This can be served as a salad or stew.

Salad Green Thoughts

Salads have great versatility. They can be one-dish meals, hearty or light, or delicate, dazzling beginnings or ends to meals. Some or all of the ingredients can be cooked and the salad assembled well before time to eat; green salads can be garnished with herbs or flowers just before serving and tossed at the table. Because the elements of salads are not cooked together to marry flavors, the texture, color, and flavor of each ingredient are important. Freshness is essential.

Whether a salad is a meal in itself or served to stimulate the appetite or refresh the palate, a balance of the four elemental tastes—salt, sweet, sour, and bitter—satisfies most completely. Greens contain mineral salts in varying degrees. You may add table salt to taste. Many greens, especially when they are very fresh, taste sweet, lettuces and cabbage notably so. Some people add a pinch of sugar to dressings to accentuate this sweetness. We like to use small amounts of ingredients such as fruit, nuts, or cheese, which contain natural sugar. A few greens, such as sorrel and purslane, are sour; as for the others, the acid in vinaigrettes or the lemon squeezed over cooked greens at the last minute provides the sour component. Quite a few greens have a bitter taste. Often, bitter and sweet tastes are combined in a complex way. Many of the mustards and chicories show this trait. If the greens have no natural bitterness, we may add it in the form of a few drops of bitters. Salt and sweet are often overemphasized in American cooking, which makes the food somewhat dull. This habit appears to be waning as Americans are discovering that they have a full set of taste buds. Salads offer the opportunity to savor all the tastes we were born with.

GREENS IN THE GARDEN

General Guidelines

Most greens are easy to grow if their needs are respected. All like a well-drained fertile soil high in organic matter. Virtually all thrive in a subacid to neutral soil, pH 6.0 to 7.0. Greens of all kinds have the best growth and flavor when they have plenty of water. When daytime temperatures are above 75°F, this usually means daily watering. Rain or overhead watering is adequate for most greens, but they encourage rust and rot in lettuces, particularly in hot weather. Drip irrigation or otherwise applying water at the base of the plants is a good way to water all greens. Mulching between plants is a great help to keep the soil moist. All greens respond well to light side applications of granular fertilizer, or foliar feeding with a water-soluble fertilizer during the growing season. Most greens thrive on nitrogen; spinach is greedy for it. Organic fertilizers and well-aged compost or manure provide nutrients without the risk of burning the plants.

There are many creatures that like greens, as well as some soil-borne diseases. To deal with these, the gardener's first resource is clear attention; a philosophical attitude. Many biological and plant-derived controls are now available to eradicate or discourage cabbage worms, aphids, flea beetles, slugs, and snails. We have found copper strip barriers to be very effective against the last two. Of all the fauna that live in gardens, only about ten percent do harm to the crops; ladybugs and other beneficial predator insects flourish where poisons are not used. Birds, rabbits, and deer love tender young greens; barriers can be effective when erected right after transplanting or germination. The only strategies that we have found to protect plants against earwigs are flashlight forays at night to dispatch them in the act, pyrethrin/rotenone spray during plague years, and finally, resignation and reseeding. Check with your County Extension Office for information about pest control in your area.

Tending a garden is a practical pleasure. We grow delicious greens, including some prize-winners, by following time-tested cultivation practices. We keep the soil high in organic matter, check plants for insect infestation and disease, dispose promptly of affected plants, and compost stalks and outer leaves after harvests. We rotate crops, growing garden cress where we grew chicory, lettuce where we grew cabbage, peas or beans where we grew spinach. In many parts of the world, these techniques are still the norm, and ensure nourishment for very large populations.

Greens that grow well in containers include radicchios and kale (in 12-inch-deep containers), lettuces, (especially small cultivars of loose-leaf and butterhead types), tat soi, New Zealand spinach, rocket, watercress, mallow, and perilla. Even small greens grow best in 10- to 12-inch-deep containers. Salad mixes would probably do well in long window boxes. We usually under- or interplant the greens with small edible flowers such as Gem marigolds, nasturtiums, and Johnny-jump-ups. Container-grown greens need close attention to water and fertilization. We plant in soilless potting mix rather than in garden soil to promote good drainage.

Greens' Seasons

Cabbages are biennials grown as annuals; they thrive in cool weather and need ample fertilization to produce large heads. Most mature in sixty to eighty days. Look for slow-bolting varieties of both Oriental and European types for spring sowings. In areas with short springs and hot summers, cabbages, as well as flowering mustards, mizuna, kale, collards, turnip greens, and lettuces may do better when grown under shade cloth. Heading Chinese cabbages are best direct-seeded and grow best from late summer/autumn sowings in USDA hardiness zones 5–9. Other kinds can be started in flats in late winter or early spring and transplanted to the garden, or from late summer/early fall direct seedings.

Kale and collards have growing requirements similar to those of cabbages. In the southern tier of the United States, they are sown in late summer to overwinter but may also yield some fall harvests. In cooler climates, they may be started in flats and transplanted to the garden, or direct-seeded in early spring. Kale and collards withstand heat without flowering better than many other brassicas. When we harvest them during the summer, we refrigerate the leaves for two or three days to bring out their sweetness. We don't remove the center leaves, as this will retard growth. Ragged Jack is particularly heat-tolerant and keeps good flavor when well watered.

Flowering mustards—broccoli di rabe, pak choi, choi sum, and tat soi—and turnip greens are best sown and transplanted in cool weather. They grow quickly then and are quite tasty even when their flowers—which are edible and delicious—have formed, as long as the plants are compact and the flowers are on short shoots. Flowering mustards will overwinter with some protection in zones 5–9. They respond well to plenty of water and fertilizer.

Mustard greens will do with somewhat less water and fertilizer than other greens. They often respond to lengthening days by bolting. For spring mustard greens, we start them in flats very early in the year and transplant them to the garden as soon as possible. As they grow well in warm and humid conditions, midsummer and early autumn are the best times to direct-seed them.

Mizuna and spinach mustard are unusual among the brassicas in that they will grow in warm weather without bolting or becoming bitter, although large leaves are tough. It is possible to make successive sowings until early summer if the plants have adequate water and filtered shade. During the summer, plants should be harvested frequently, when leaves are an inch or so long for salads, or 2 to 3 inches long for cooking. In cool weather or warm, just the outer leaves may be harvested, or entire plants may be cut to about an inch from the ground; these will resprout.

Turnip greens, and turnips, grow successfully only in cool weather. We transplant Tyfon seedlings to the garden in early spring for a brief crop of greens but sow it and other nonrooting turnips in late summer to harvest about six weeks later.

Curly endive and escarole need about three months to produce large heads, but we have very tender crops of these for about two months from late winter/early spring sowings. When grown close together, the plants will self-blanch as long as there is not too much overhead water to cause disease. We harvest the first curly endive by shearing it, let small heads form and self-blanch, then harvest whole heads. Outer leaves of young escarole, about 3 inches tall, are delicious. After harvesting outer leaves, loose heads will form, which may stay sweet or turn bitter, depending on heat, but most kinds can be cut back continually. We have had good luck with the Batavian cultivars. Endive and escarole do not germinate well in warm weather, but spring-sown plants can be left through the summer, and the outer leaves cut back for cooking; heads will form when daytime temperatures reach the low 60s. The cool weather will

Above: Shepherd's piquant salad mix combines spicy greens—arugula, red mustard, and cress—with mild mizuna for balance.

sweeten them; the inner leaves can be sweetened further by tying up the outer leaves. Endive and escarole will not overwinter unprotected except in Zone 10, but they can take a little frost and will grow in a cold frame, or other protected situations, yielding early and sweet salads in the spring.

Radicchios, like other chicories, are not as demanding of water and fer-

Chicory in the garden.

tilizer as most other greens. The blanching radicchios grow best in fine and well-drained soil, which fosters the large and deep roots needed to produce good heads. We sow Castelfranco, Treviso, and Verona in spring for fall harvest, thinning to about 8 inches between plants. We harvest some early outer leaves for salad, then keep the plants cut back to 6 to 10 inches during the summer. When the nights begin to cool, 60°F or below, we cover the plants with flowerpots or homemade, well-ventilated black plastic cloches. The time required for full-hearted, well-colored heads to form is generally three weeks, depending on the temperature. In mild climates, garden radicchios may also be forced by overwintering. After you have harvested fall heads, cover the stumps with 6 inches or so of well-aged compost or a mixture of compost and as much as 50 percent soil. New heads will form in early spring. Radicchios can also be sown midsummer, but germination is erratic.

You can force radicchios out of season, if you have an extra refrigerator that is not opened much. Dig up plants with roots at least an inch in diameter. Trim roots back to 6 inches and leaves to about 2 inches. Place the plants in ventilated plastic bags. Cover the roots with soilless potting mix, close the bags loosely, and store in single layers. With this method, softball-sized heads form in about two months. The larger the roots, the larger the heads will be. The flavor is not as fine as that of plants blanched in the ground. For a discussion of non- or self-blanching types, see page 20.

Dutch savoy cabbage growing in a summer garden.

Spinach grows quickly in spring and fall, maturing from direct-sown seed in about six weeks. For the deepest green leaves and healthiest plants, fertilize weekly with light side applications of granular fertilizer, manure or compost tea, or foliar fertilizer. Spinach is perpetually thirsty; we have never been able to overwater it. Spinach bolts readily with heat and long days; some bolt-resistant cultivars have been developed. We grow it and beet greens, which have similar nutrient and water requirements, during cool weather, and harvest other greens during the summer. Spinach thrives in well-drained soil with plenty of organic matter. New Zealand spinach can be seeded in late spring/early summer and prefers sandy, loamy soil.

Chard is one of our summer mainstay greens. It is slower to mature than spinach or beet greens (about sixty-five days from direct sowings), but makes up for this by producing during hot weather as long as it is well watered, and fed every two or three weeks. Harvest mature outer leaves, taking care not to damage center leaves. Chard seems to like frequent thinning, sending out new growth that matures quickly. In very mild climates, zones 9–10, it may produce for several years if harvested regularly and cut back in late fall.

After attempting to sow lettuces once a week for succession crops during the summer, and trying several summer varieties, we now grow lettuces only in cool weather. Germination is very spotty in direct-seeded lettuce when temperatures are above 65°F, and in our experience, lettuces do not transplant well. The best way we've found to extend our lettuce salads is to sow slow-bolting varieties, sow late in spring only if daytime temperatures are around 60°F, and to give the plants some filtered shade. Loose-leafed types seem slower to bolt, particularly Oak Leaf and Salad Bowl. Shade can be provided by shade cloth, or by placing the lettuce under corn, or in the shade of other tall plants. Even fall- and spring-grown lettuce needs ample water, preferably not overhead, as the delicate leaves are prone to rotting and other diseases and pests when kept too wet.

Heat and long days—summer—cause rocket to become very strong, even bitter. If it germinates at all, it will offer two or three leaves and send up flower stalks immediately. During cool weather, rocket is very easy to grow, adapting to less-than-perfect soil, little water, and no fertilizer. Once it has been grown in a place that it likes, it will reseed readily.

Watercress can be grown from seed, or it can be easily rooted from fresh spring supermarket watercress, then grown in soilless potting mix in containers. It likes fresh water daily from the bottom and prefers filtered shade. When it flowers, the leaves will be somewhat bitter. Upland cress is grown like watercress. Garden cress is as easy to grow as radishes. It prefers cool weather, but repeated harvesting will extend its season from late spring sowings.

Sorrel is undemanding in the garden. It has the best flavor in cool weather and when well watered. Plants produce well for several years in fertile soil. The leaves will yellow and die back in summer if in full sun; place plants in partial shade and keep flower stalks cut back to harvest sorrel during the summer.

Bok choi (Brassica rapa, Chinensis Group) is also called pak choi.

Perilla is an annual that reseeds to the point of weediness in some situations. It prefers well-drained fertile soil and tolerates heat and humidity when it has ample water. For best flavor and abundance, we grow it with moderate fertilization and frequent harvests. We cut entire young plants for cooking or prune plants to keep them branching and bushy. Pinching out flower buds as they form will keep leaves coming.

Salad mixes are grown like lettuces, during cool weather in spring and fall. Commercial mixes have the advantage of fairly similar and consistent germination times, and the disadvantage of having the same set of flavors for each sowing. In addition to growing packaged mixes, we sow mini-beds of varieties whose flavors we like together and with other salad plants. These are made of seeds sown separately in short (10- to 12-inch) narrow (2- to 3-inch) rows. Germination times should be close so that varieties may be harvested together. In early spring, we like to sow these mini-beds with frisée, rocket, corn salad, and cutting chicory. In mid- or late spring, we sow mini-beds or make a mix of colored loose-leaf lettuce, escarole, perhaps a nonforcing radicchio, purslane, and dill or coriander. Purslane is a little slow, but it is ready midseason.

Whether you sow packaged mixes or make your own, it is wise to buy seed from specialty houses that give germination times on the packets. Choose kinds that germinate within a day or two of one another. Though we advocate experimentation, we can counsel against what a friend did: do *not* go to the local hardware or garden supply store and choose a number of attractive salad seed packages, take them home, mix them all together, and sow them. What will come will not be mesclun, but according to what you have chosen, the seed company, and the weather, a stand of green loose-leaf lettuce, a patch of gar-

den cress, or nothing at all until fall, when a few surviving chicories decide that it's cool enough to germinate.

Amaranth is heat tolerant, frost-tender, and prefers well-drained, fertile soil and full sun. Keep the plants pruned to promote branching and delay flowering. Amaranth is extremely productive; it can be harvested by picking leaves, pruning tops, or pulling tender plants.

Chrysanthemum requires very good drainage, and a position in filtered shade in hot climates. It is traditionally, and best, a spring green. Buds can be pinched back for more leaf production, but when you tire of chrysanthemum salad, stir-fry, and tea in the spring, you can let the flowers form for a handsome summer display.

Corn salad wants the best situation and care in the salad garden; sunshine, abundant water, rich, fertile, loamy soil. Unlike most other cool-season greens, corn salad needs some warmth to germinate, though it grows best in cool conditions and is quite frost-hardy. We have gotten the best germination when the daytime air temperature was about 60°F. This means sowing in late summer or early or late fall, depending on how mild your winters are. Established plants do quite well through mild winters, covered with mulch if necessary, and make a great spring showing. If your winters are very mild (zones 9–10), late winter and very early spring sowings will produce good crops. In colder climates, corn salad can be grown in flats and transplanted out as soon as possible. Of the many kinds we have grown, we have had particularly high germination with Coquille.

Sow dandelion in the fall and harvest in late winter or early spring, after the greens have been sweetened by cold weather. For salads, 3- to 6-inch leaves are best; larger greens can be blanched and cooked. Do not allow the plants to flower in late spring; they will be bitter, and you will have more dandelions than you want. As you may have noticed, dandelion does not need any special care.

Good-King-Henry is a perennial that is evergreen in mild climates, while lamb's-quarters is an annual that will pop up all over your garden if you are not careful to keep seed from setting. Both flourish in well-drained soils, providing many leaves to cook alone or with other greens. They do not require the highly fertile soil that most other greens do, but do like water during the summer. In hot summers Good-King-Henry will die back; keep it watered for a nice flush of fall growth.

Orach has a central stalk with many branches and shoots and so it is a good provider in small spaces. Some varieties can grow to 6 feet tall though not much more than 12 inches in diameter; we harvest orach regularly to keep plants short and bushy. It produces best in cool weather but will give some early summer harvests if well watered. Where temperatures shoot up quickly, so will orach, bolting into very decorative flowers and eventually seedpods.

The Greens Book

R E C I P E S

APPETIZERS AND FIRST COURSES

BAKED SPINACH AND PARMESAN GNOCCHI

This is a variation of gnocchi verdi, a very old dish from central Italy. The gnocchi, little pasta, were traditionally made with ricotta cheese and poached. These green gnocchi are baked and simple to make. They disappear so quickly that you may want to make a double batch and freeze one batch after you have formed them. Bake frozen gnocchi for 20 to 25 minutes, turning them two or three times. We usually serve these as an appetizer; they are also good as a first course with a light tomato sauce.

SERVES 6 TO 12

1 large onion, diced fine
3 garlic cloves, minced
4 tablespoons (60 ml) butter
2 pounds (900 g) spinach, washed and trimmed of large stems
3 eggs
2 egg whites
1 cup (240 ml) freshly grated parmesan cheese
1 1/2 to 2 cups (360 to 475 ml) fine dry bread crumbs
Freshly grated nutmeg
Salt and freshly ground pepper

In a sauté pan, soften the onion and garlic in the butter. Remove the pan from the heat and let it stand, uncovered. While the onion and garlic are cooking, place the washed and trimmed spinach in a colander and drain 10 minutes.

Place the damp spinach in a large noncorrodible pot, cover, and cook over medium-high heat. When you hear the water sizzling, remove the cover and stir the spinach until it is just wilted. Place the spinach in a colander and cool to room temperature.

Preheat the oven to 350°F (180°C) and butter two large baking sheets. Thoroughly squeeze the excess water from the spinach leaves and chop them fine.

Place the spinach in a large bowl along with the softened onion and garlic, eggs and egg whites, parmesan, and bread crumbs. Season the mixture well with nutmeg, salt, and pepper, and mix thoroughly. For easier rolling, you may chill the mixture, tightly covered, for 15 minutes or as long as 24 hours.

Roll the mixture into 3/4-inch balls and place them on the baking sheets. Bake the gnocchi about 15 minutes, turning once, until they are lightly browned. Serve hot.

RED CABBAGE AND FONTINA TOASTS

We devised this Italian-style toasted bread and vegetable appetizer for late fall and winter, when cabbage is fresh and tomatoes, peppers, and eggplant are out of season. It is called crostone—big toast—in Italian and is good before rustic soups and stews, roast chicken, duck, breast of veal, and sausages.

SERVES 4 TO 6

1/2 small head red cabbage, about 1/2 pound (225 g)
1 red onion, about 6 ounces (170 g)
1/3 cup (80 ml) extra-virgin olive oil
3 garlic cloves, minced
About 1 tablespoon (15 ml) red wine vinegar
Salt and freshly ground black pepper
6 slices good country bread 3/4 inch (2 cm) thick
6 ounces (170 g) Italian fontina or taleggio cheese
1 to 2 garlic cloves, peeled
2 tablespoons (30 ml) chopped Italian parsley for garnish

Rinse, halve, and core the cabbage. Slice it very thin. Halve the onion and slice it very thin. Heat 2 tablespoons (30 ml) of the olive oil in a large noncorrodible sauté pan over medium heat. Add the cabbage and onion and toss well to coat with oil. Cook the vegetables for 5 minutes.

Stir in the garlic and vinegar and season lightly with salt and pepper. Cover the pan and cook for about 5 minutes, until the vegetables are just soft. Adjust the seasoning if necessary.

Meanwhile, brush the bread slices on both sides with olive oil and toast them in a 400°F (200°C) oven for about 10 minutes, turning them once. While the bread is toasting, cut the cheese into 1/2-inch (1-cm) strips and toss with the remaining olive oil. Remove the toast from the oven when it is crusty on both sides and rub it on one side with a garlic clove.

Cut the toast in half diagonally. Put a layer of cabbage on the each piece. Arrange the cheese over the cabbage on a diagonal, leaving about 1/2 inch (1 cm) of space between the strips.

Preheat the oven to broil. Place the crostone on a baking sheet and broil 3 inches (8 cm) from the heat for 1 to 2 minutes, or until the cheese bubbles and browns slightly.

Sprinkle the chopped parsley between the cheese strips and serve immediately.

PIZZA WITH ESCAROLE AND MOZZARELLA

Green pizza? We can't guarantee that this will be a hit with the children, but it certainly has been with the many adults we've served it to. This is a good dough for any pizza topping; the texture is even better if the dough has a slow, cool rise in the refrigerator overnight. It can be made ahead, divided into convenient portions, and packed into oiled, airtight freezer bags after kneading. Place in the freezer immediately. Thaw at room temperature before shaping and topping. We once discovered an 8-month-old bag of dough in the freezer, which made an excellent pizza. The optimum maximum storage time is 3 to 4 months. We take the dough from the freezer at breakfast time, leave it at room temperature all day, and have pizza for dinner.

MAKES TWO 12-INCH PIZZAS
SERVES 8 TO 12 AS AN APPETIZER, 4 TO 6 AS A MAIN COURSE

PIZZA DOUGH
2 teaspoons (10 ml) active dry yeast
1½ cups (360 ml) water
3½ cups (830 ml) unbleached white flour
1/2 cup (120 ml) whole wheat flour, or use another 1/2 cup (120 ml) white flour
2 tablespoons (30 ml) olive oil
1 teaspoon (5 ml) salt

Dissolve the yeast in 1/4 cup (60 ml) warm (100–105°F; 47–50°C) water. When the yeast has softened and become foamy, in about 10 minutes, add it to the rest of the water.

Mix the flours in a bowl and make a well in the center. Gradually stir the water and yeast into the well. Add the olive oil and salt. Gather the dough and knead it for 7 or 8 minutes, or until is is soft and lively.

Let the dough double in bulk in a lightly oiled, covered bowl. Divide the dough into two parts. Cover them with a damp towel and let them relax by resting, covered, for 30 minutes to an hour. Preheat the oven to 400°F (200°C).

ESCAROLE TOPPING

1 large bunch escarole, about 1¼ pounds (560 g)
2 garlic cloves, chopped fine
2 tablespoons (30 ml) olive oil
1/4 pound (115 g) mozzarella cheese, cut in small dice
1 cup (240 ml) freshly grated pecorino, romano, or parmesan cheese
Salt and pepper
Red pepper flakes, optional
Cornmeal or semolina
Olive oil

Wash the escarole and dry it well. Discard the large stems. Shred the rest, and mix with the garlic.

Heat the olive oil over medium heat in a large sauté pan. Add the escarole and cook it about 5 minutes, or until just wilted. Transfer the escarole to a mixing bowl to cool.

When the dough has relaxed, stretch one portion gently to about half the size of your pizza pan. Sprinkle the pan with cornmeal or semolina, or rub it lightly with olive oil. Place the stretched dough in the pan and finish stretching it to just over the rim of the pan. If you have two pizza pans and enough oven space to bake the pizzas at the same time, prepare the dough for both.

Add the cheeses to the escarole mixture and season with salt, pepper, and red pepper flakes, if desired. Mix well. Brush the dough in the pan lightly with olive oil. Spread half of the escarole mixture on each prepared dough.

Bake the pizza for 20 to 25 minutes. Remove from the oven and brush the rim lightly with olive oil. Remove the pizza from the pan and let it stand for 3 to 4 minutes before cutting. Prepare and bake the other pizza if you have not done so. Serve hot or warm.

ANCHO CORN PUDDING WITH WILTED GREENS

This chile-flavored pudding, bursting with sweet corn kernels and served on a bed of wilted, slightly bitter greens dressed with a little vinegar, provides the palate with many flavor nuances and has an interesting texture as well. The dish is best served hot or warm, though it can also be served at room temperature. Use greens from your garden or whatever looks good at the market; we usually use equal parts of spinach, chard, and purple mustard greens. Serve this as an appetizer, a vegetable side dish, or a light main course with warm tortillas.

SERVES 4 TO 8

1 1/2 cups (360 ml) milk

1 large dried ancho chile, about 1 ounce (30 g), stemmed and seeded and cut in 1/4-inch (5-mm) dice

8 very small mustard or spinach leaves

2 tablespoons (30 ml) unsalted butter

1 cup (240 ml) chopped Vidalia or other sweet onion

2 cups (475 ml) fresh corn kernels, or frozen corn kernels, thawed

Salt and freshly ground black pepper

1 1/2 tablespoons (22 ml) cornmeal

1 1/2 tablespoons (22 ml) unbleached flour

3 extra-large eggs, lightly beaten

1 cup (240 ml) grated sharp white cheddar cheese

1 1/2 pounds (675 g) assorted greens, such as spinach, chard, and mustard, washed, with large stems removed

Handful of fresh lamb's-quarters or epazote leaves

1 large garlic clove, minced

1 to 1 1/2 tablespoons (15 to 22 ml) olive oil

1 to 2 teaspoons (5 to 10 ml) red wine or sherry vinegar

Place the milk and ancho chile in a noncorrodible saucepan and scald. Remove from the heat and let stand for 20 to 30 minutes.

Preheat the oven to 375°F (190°C). Generously butter eight 5- to 6-ounce (140- to 170-ml) custard cups or ramekins. Line the bottom and the sides of molds with the small mustard or spinach leaves.

Melt the butter in a small sauté pan over medium heat and sauté the onion for about 5 minutes, stirring occasionally. Add the corn and sauté 2 to 3 minutes longer. Season with salt and pepper and sprinkle the cornmeal and flour over all. Stir well, cook for 1 or 2 minutes, and remove from heat.

Add the eggs to the scalded ancho milk and pour this into the corn mixture; add the cheese and combine well. Spoon the batter into the prepared molds, taking care to distribute the vegetables and liquid evenly.

Place the filled molds in a shallow pan. Pour about 2 cups (475 ml) of hot water into the pan. Place it in the preheated oven and bake for 18 to 20 minutes, or until the pudding is set.

While the pudding is baking, chop the greens coarse and put them in a large non-corrodible pot. Add about 1/4 cup (60 ml) water, cover the pot, and wilt the greens over medium heat for about 5 minutes, stirring occasionally. Add the garlic, olive oil, vinegar, salt, and pepper and stir over low heat for 2 or 3 minutes. Taste and add a little more salt, pepper, oil, or vinegar, if necessary. Remove the pan from the heat.

When the puddings are done, remove them from the oven. Arrange the greens evenly on four or eight plates. Run a metal spatula around the edges of each custard cup and turn the puddings out onto the greens. Serve hot, warm, or at room temperature.

Perilla is a favorite sushi and potherb in Japan, where it is known as shiso. Here it is rolled around an omelet to make a tasty vegetarian roll. It is good with other sushi fillings, particularly tuna, cucumber, and avocado. Use green or purple perilla, or try the cumin-scented variety for added flavor. Serve the sushi with dipping bowls of soy sauce and little plates of wasabi and pickled ginger for garnish.

MAKES ABOUT 40 SUSHI

1 cup (240 ml) sweet or short-grain Oriental rice
1¼ cups (300 ml) water
2 extra-large eggs
1 teaspoon (5 ml) water
Salt and freshly ground pepper
1/2 teaspoon (2 ml) sugar
1 teaspoon (5 ml) sesame seeds
Scant 1 teaspoon (5 ml) peanut or vegetable oil
Scant 1/2 teaspoon (2 ml) salt
2 tablespoons (30 ml) rice vinegar
1 tablespoon (15 ml) water
1 teaspoon (5 ml) sugar
About 1/2 teaspoon (2 ml) dark sesame oil
5 sheets nori seaweed
About 6 large perilla leaves, halved lengthwise, with stems removed, or 12 smaller ones
Soy sauce, wasabi, and pickled ginger

Wash and rinse the rice if necessary. Combine the rice and water in a noncorrodible pan and bring them to a boil. Cover, reduce the heat to a simmer, and cook for 25 minutes. Remove from heat and let stand, covered, for about 10 minutes. Remove the lid from the pan and let the rice cool until it is just warm.

While the rice is cooking, prepare the omelet. Beat the eggs with 1 teaspoon water in a small bowl and stir the salt, pepper, sugar and sesame seeds into them. Heat the peanut or vegetable oil in a small sauté pan over moderate heat. Add the egg mixture and cook until the bottom is light golden brown. Loosen the omelet from the pan with a spatula and flip it over. Cook the omelet on the other side until it is just set. Remove it from the pan and cool it on a plate. When the omelet is cool, cut it into 1/2-inch strips. Wrap the perilla leaves around the omelet strips.

In a small bowl, mix the salt, vinegar, 1 tablespoon water, sugar, and sesame oil. Sprinkle the mixture over the rice and toss well.

Toast the nori by quickly passing the glossy side over a medium flame. Lay one sheet on a bamboo mat, glossy side down, with a short side facing you. Moisten your fingertips with water and rub them lightly over the seaweed.

Divide the rice into five portions, one for each sushi roll. Spread half of one portion in a strip about 1 inch (2 cm) wide across the lower third of the nori. Place one or two perilla-wrapped omelet strips down the center of the rice. Cover the omelet with the other half portion of rice.

Begin rolling by bringing the edge of the sheet closest to you over the rice, using the mat to guide the roll. Continue until the roll is complete; hold the mat in place for 30 seconds to set the sushi. Make the remaining rolls in the same way. Cut each roll with a sharp knife into 1-inch (2-cm) slices. Serve immediately or cover tightly with plastic wrap and refrigerate for up to 24 hours. Bring to cool room temperature before serving.

RADICCHIO AND BEAN SALAD

In this dramatic salad, the variegated rose and pale green of Castelfranco or the burgundy of Verona or Treviso radicchio provide high contrast to the ivory beans and black olives. Cannellini beans are preferred as they hold their shape well when completely cooked, as beans should be, and they have a fine, creamy texture.

SERVES 6 TO 8

8 ounces (225 g) dry cannellini or other small white beans
4 to 5 tablespoons (60 to 75 ml) extra-virgin olive oil
2 to 3 tablespoons (30 to 45 ml) red wine vinegar
Salt and freshly ground black pepper
12 ounces (340 g) radicchio, preferably Castelfranco
1/2 small sweet white onion, sliced thin
12 to 15 Gaeta or Kalamata olives, pitted and halved

Soak the beans overnight in water to cover, or soften by boiling for 5 minutes, then soaking for an hour. Drain beans, cover with ample water, and simmer until just done. Drain, reserving water for another use if desired.

While the beans are still warm, season with about two-thirds of the olive oil, vinegar, salt, and pepper.

Wash and trim the radicchio and tear it into bite-sized pieces.

Arrange the radicchio on a platter and drizzle with the remaining olive oil and vinegar. Season with salt and pepper. Arrange the beans on top. Scatter sliced onion and olives over the salad. Just before serving, toss everything together and adjust the seasoning.

BRUSCHETTA WITH ARUGULA AND BALSAMIC TOMATOES

A winning summertime combination—arugula and tomatoes—on toasted garlic bread is the perfect way to start a meal. For small appetizers, you may slice a baguette into rounds. The instructions here yield large, rustic appetizers, one per person. If you serve these as a main course for lunch, allow two per person. Imported olives make a nice accompaniment.

SERVES 4 OR 8

1 pint (475 ml) cherry or pear tomatoes, quartered lengthwise and halved crosswise
About 4 tablespoons (60 ml) extra-virgin olive oil
1 tablespoon (15 ml) balsamic vinegar
1 garlic clove, minced
2 tablespoons (30 ml) chopped chives or garlic chives
Salt and freshly ground pepper
1 long baguette or 4 long rolls, each 6 to 8 inches (15 to 20 cm) long
2 cups (475 ml) washed arugula, chopped coarse if leaves are large
1 to 2 garlic cloves, peeled
3/4 to 1 cup (180 to 240 ml) grated mozzarella cheese, optional

Combine the tomatoes in a bowl with 2 tablespoons (30 ml) of the olive oil, vinegar, minced garlic, and chives. Salt and pepper generously and toss well.

Cut the baguette into four pieces, 6 to 8 inches (15 to 20 cm) long. Slice the baguette pieces or the rolls in half lengthwise and place them on a baking sheet. Toast them in a 400°F (200°C) oven for about 10 minutes, turning them once. While the bread is toasting, add the arugula to the tomatoes and toss well.

Remove the toast from the oven when it is crusty on both sides and rub the cut sides with a clove of garlic. Brush the cut sides with the remaining olive oil.

If you are using mozzarella, scatter it evenly over the toasted garlic bread and place the bread under the broiler for about 2 minutes, or until the cheese just melts. Spoon the tomato and arugula mixture evenly over the baguettes, and drizzle a little of the marinade juices over all. Serve immediately.

SOUPS AND PASTAS

POTATO ARUGULA SOUP

Arugula has been used in Mediterranean cooking for thousands of years. It is one of the many herbs that people who work the land have foraged as well as cultivated. This soup is made with water rather than broth or stock, which points to its simple origins. It is flavorful and quick to make, an excellent dish for early spring when the garden is full of arugula that must be harvested, and when markets have an abundance of it. Field cress and broadleaf cress may be substituted; their flavor is good but does not have the special tang that arugula has.

SERVES 4 TO 6
6 large garlic cloves
1 small dried red chile pepper
2 tablespoons (30 ml) olive oil
2½ pounds (1.1 kg) russet potatoes
1 pound (450 g) arugula, washed and trimmed of large stems
6 cups (about 1½ liters) water
Salt and freshly ground pepper
4 to 6 soup-plate-sized slices of country bread
Olive oil
1 cup (240 ml) freshly grated pecorino romano cheese

Chop five of the garlic cloves coarse. In a soup pot over low heat, soften the garlic and chile pepper in 2 tablespoons (30 ml) olive oil.

Meanwhile, peel the potatoes and cut them into bite-sized chunks. When the garlic is soft, add the potatoes and water to the pot. Bring to a boil and cook uncovered over medium heat for 10 minutes.

If arugula leaves are large, 5 to 6 inches (14 to 15 cm) long, chop them coarse. Add arugula to potatoes and reduce the heat slightly. Season well with salt and pepper.

Cook the soup until the potatoes have partially disintegrated, stirring occasionally and breaking them up a bit.

Toast the bread to make croutons. Rub each slice well with the remaining garlic clove. Brush lightly with olive oil. Place the croutons in soup plates and sprinkle with the cheese.

When ready to serve the soup, discard the red pepper and adjust the seasoning. Ladle over the croutons and serve immediately.

Black-Eyed Pea, Kale, and Turnip Green Soup

Two regional favorites from the southern United States are black-eyed peas and greens. We like them together in this hearty, tasty, good-for-you soup. This is a meatless version; if you love the flavor of ham with greens, add a ham bone to the peas while they are cooking. You may use all kale, all turnip, all collard greens, or a combination of greens. Serve the soup with cornbread, of course.

SERVES 6

1 pound (450 g) black-eyed peas, soaked for at least 4 hours, or overnight
1 teaspoon (5 ml) salt
2½ tablespoons (38 ml) olive oil
About 12 ounces (340 g) mixed kale and turnip greens
1 large red onion, chopped
3 large garlic cloves, minced
2 cups (475 ml) vegetable or chicken stock
1/2 to 1 teaspoon (2 to 5 ml) Tabasco
1 roasted red bell pepper, peeled, seeded, and diced, about 2/3 cup (160 ml)
Salt and freshly ground pepper

Drain and rinse the peas and place them in a noncorrodible pot. Cover them with 2 inches (5 cm) water and add the salt and 1½ teaspoons (8 ml) olive oil. Cook the peas over moderate heat for 40 to 45 minutes, or until they are almost tender. Meanwhile, wash the greens, discard large stems, and tear or chop the leaves into large bite-sized pieces. Chop the smaller stems into 1/2-inch (1-cm) pieces.

In a small pan, sauté the chopped stems, onion, and garlic in the remaining olive oil in a small pan over medium heat for about 5 minutes. Add them to the peas along with the greens, stock, and Tabasco and cook for 10 minutes. Add the bell pepper and season with salt and pepper. Cook about 5 minutes longer, or until peas and greens are done. Adjust the seasoning and serve hot.

Naples-Style Cabbage and Endive Soup

Greens have a definite affinity for ham, as people from China to Italy have known for centuries. In this light yet flavorful winter soup from Naples, a prosciutto bone or ends add a special flavor, but any unsmoked ham bone could be used. Pancetta—Italian-style unsmoked bacon rolled with pepper—adds some cured pork flavor. Savoy cabbage and two kinds of endive become mellow and satisfying even when they are cooked without ham broth.

Serves 6 to 8

1 prosciutto bone, or about 1/3 pound (150 g) prosciutto ends, if available

2 quarts (2 liters) water

1/2 pound (225 g) Italian sausage

1/4 pound (115 g) pancetta, sliced about 1/8 inch (3 mm) thick

1 tablespoon (15 ml) olive oil

1 onion, diced

1 celery rib, diced

1 carrot, diced

1 garlic clove, minced

About 1¼ pounds (560 g) Savoy cabbage

12 ounces (340 g) Belgian endive

12 ounces (340 g) escarole or curly endive

1 to 2½ quarts (1 to 2½ liters) chicken stock

Salt and freshly ground pepper

Freshly grated parmesan cheese

Simmer the prosciutto bone or ends covered in the water for about 2 hours. Discard the bone or ends and reserve the stock.

Crumble or slice the sausage and dice the pancetta. Render the meats over low heat for about 15 minutes, or until the pancetta is somewhat crisp. Drain the fat from the meat and place the meat on a plate.

Add the olive oil, onion, celery, carrot, and garlic to the pan in which the meats were rendered. Soften the vegetables over low heat and transfer them to a soup pot.

Trim the cabbage, endive, and escarole of tough outer leaves and wash well. Cut the vegetables into quarters lengthwise, discarding ribs and cores, then across in about 1/2-inch (1-cm) slices.

Place the vegetables in the soup pot. Add the prosciutto stock and 1 quart (1 liter)

chicken stock, or use 2½ quarts (2½ liters) chicken stock. Simmer the soup for 15 minutes.

Add the sausage and pancetta to the pot. Simmer the soup for another 10 minutes or so. Adjust the seasoning and serve hot, with parmesan cheese in a separate dish for garnish.

FETTUCCINE WITH ROCKET, CRESS, AND GOAT CHEESE

As a simple, quick, and flavorful spring pasta dish, this one is hard to beat. We have been making versions of it for a dozen years; this is our current favorite.

SERVES 4 TO 6

1 cup (240 ml) whipping cream (double cream)
1 cup (240 ml) half-and-half (single cream)
3 garlic cloves, minced
About 5 ounces (140 ml) mild goat cheese
1 pound (450 ml) fresh fettuccine
1 cup (240 ml) rocket leaves, chopped coarse
1 cup (240 ml) watercress leaves, or leaves and tender stems of curly or broadleaf cress
Salt and freshly ground pepper

Combine the whipping cream, half-and-half, and garlic in a large sauté pan. Bring them to a boil, reduce the heat, and cook over medium-low heat for about 5 minutes to reduce slightly.

Reduce the heat to low and crumble the goat cheese into the sauce. Cook, stirring occasionally, about 3 minutes, or until the cheese melts. Remove the sauce from the heat.

Cook the fettuccine in a large pot of boiling salted water until tender but still slightly firm. Drain the pasta.

Stir the rocket and cress into the sauce and season with salt and pepper. Toss the fettuccine with the sauce. Transfer to a heated platter or pasta dishes and serve hot with a grinding of black pepper on top.

For a change, begin by softening a shallot or two in a tablespoon of butter. Then add the creams, omitting the garlic, and proceed with the recipe.

CABBAGE POTATO CARAWAY SOUP WITH CROUTONS AND GOUDA

This is a flavorful, satisfying fall and winter dinner soup. We often prepare a vegetable tray with radishes, onions, celery stalks, pickled beets or cornichons, and perhaps some hard-cooked eggs as an accompaniment. We make extra croutons for those who like to dunk bread in their soup and offer cold beer to drink.

SERVES 4 TO 6

2 tablespoons (30 ml) olive oil
1 large Vidalia or other sweet onion, quartered lengthwise and sliced crosswise
1½ teaspoons (8 ml) caraway seed, ground coarse
1 pound red-skinned potatoes, quartered lengthwise, and sliced 1/4 inch (5 mm) thick
3 large garlic cloves, minced
1 teaspoon (5 ml) Hungarian paprika
1 pound (450 g) cabbage, chopped coarse
6 cups (1½ liters) vegetable or chicken stock
About 1 teaspoon (5 ml) salt
2 teaspoons (10 ml) Dijon-style mustard
Freshly ground pepper
1 garlic clove, peeled
About 1 cup (240 ml) grated gouda cheese
6 to 12 slices country-style white or rye bread with caraway, about 3/8 inch (8 mm) thick

In a large, noncorrodible pot, heat the oil over moderate heat and sauté the onion for 3 to 4 minutes. Add the caraway seed, potatoes, and garlic and sauté, stirring occasionally, for 4 minutes. Add the paprika and half of the cabbage, and cook for 3 minutes longer.

Add the stock and salt, cover, and bring to a boil. Reduce the heat to a simmer and cook 12 to 15 minutes, or until the potatoes are tender.

Purée a generous half of the soup with a little of the broth in a blender or food processor in batches and return the purée to the soup pot. Stir in the remaining cabbage and mustard and season with salt and pepper. Cover and cook for 6 to 7 minutes over low heat, or until the cabbage is crisp-tender. Taste for seasoning.

While the soup is cooking, toast the bread in a toaster. Rub the bread on both sides with a clove of garlic. Cut the toast into pieces 2½ to 3 inches (6 to 8 cm) wide.

Preheat the broiler. Ladle the hot soup into ovenproof bowls. Place 1 or 2 croutons in each bowl and cover them with the grated cheese. Place the bowls on a baking sheet and put them under the broiler for 1 to 2 minutes, or until the cheese is melted. Serve immediately.

PENNE WITH BROCCOLI RABE, PINE NUTS, AND CURRANTS

Other robust greens such as Chinese flowering broccoli or flowering mustard (sometimes called galuzzi or galizzi) may be used in place of the broccoli rabe; the flavor will be different and interesting. Double the recipe to serve as a main course for 6 to 8 people. Add as much garlic as your group likes.

SERVES 3 TO 6

1 to 1¼ pounds (450 to 560 g) broccoli rabe
1/2 pound (225 g) penne or other short tubular pasta
3 tablespoons (45 ml) olive oil
4 large garlic cloves, minced
1/3 cup (80 ml) currants, soaked in warm water until plump and drained
1/3 cup (80 ml) pine nuts (pignoli), lightly toasted
Red pepper flakes, optional
Salt
Freshly grated pecorino romano or parmesan cheese

Wash the broccoli rabe well and separate the large stems from the tender stems and leaves.

Bring several quarts (liters) of water to a boil. Blanch the large stems for about 1½ minutes, until barely tender. Add tender stems and leaves and blanch 1 minute. Remove the greens to a colander to drain.

Salt the greens water and add the pasta. While the pasta cooks, heat the oil in a large sauté pan over medium-low heat. Add the garlic and soften it. Stir the greens into the garlic oil and remove from heat.

When the pasta is cooked al dente, add the currants, pine nuts, and red pepper flakes to the greens. Scoop the pasta from the water with a pasta scoop or sieve and transfer it to the pan of greens. Leave some water clinging to the pasta.

Place the pan over high heat and toss the pasta with the greens. Add one-quarter cup or so of the greens/pasta water. Add a little more salt if desired. Serve the pasta hot, accompanied by freshly grated cheese.

Greens-Filled Tortelli with
Sage Butter and Walnuts

This recipe was inspired by a wonderful tortelli dish filled with chard from *The Splendid Table*, by Lynne Rossetto Kasper. Filled tortelli are delicious no matter what combination of greens is used; experiment with whatever is in your garden. Our filling has more greens and less cheese than most ricotta-based ones; it can be made in advance and refrigerated until you are ready to fill the pasta. The simple herb and nut sauce enhances the flavor of the tortelli and is a nice change from tomato or cream sauces.

SERVES 6 TO 8

1 pound (450 g) dandelion greens, washed, stems removed
1/2 pound (225 g) beet greens, washed, stems removed
2 garlic cloves, minced
1/2 pound (225 g) ricotta cheese
1 cup (240 ml) freshly grated parmesan cheese
Freshly grated nutmeg to taste
1 extra-large egg
Salt and freshly ground pepper
1 recipe Egg Pasta (follows)
1/2 cup (120 ml) unsalted butter
16 to 20 sage leaves
1/3 cup (80 ml) toasted walnuts, chopped coarse

Place the dandelion and beet greens with the water that clings to their leaves in a non-corrodible pot. Cover and cook over moderate heat for 4 to 5 minutes, or until the greens are wilted. Transfer the greens to a colander and drain well. When cool enough to handle, squeeze out excess liquid. Chop fine.

Place the greens, garlic, ricotta and parmesan cheese, and nutmeg in a bowl. Add the egg to the mixture and season well with salt and pepper. Blend well. Refrigerate the filling covered until ready to use. Put a large pot of water on to boil for the pasta.

Prepare the egg pasta as directed. Fold the pasta gently in half lengthwise to guide your placement of the filling, then unfold the pasta. Place heaping teaspoons (8 to 10 ml) of filling along the mark in the dough, 1½ to 2 inches (4 to 5 cm) apart. Moisten the pasta lightly with water around the filling and fold it over the filling, pressing to release all air. Using a crimper-cutter, cut the tortelli into rectangles 1 to 1½ inches (2 to 4 cm) wide by 2 to 2½ inches (5 to 6 cm) long. Place the tortelli on baking sheets so that they do not touch and cover with tea towels. (Continue rolling, filling, and cutting until the pasta and filling are used up.)

Melt the butter in a sauté pan. Leave very small sage leaves whole; stack large sage leaves and cut them crosswise into shreds. When the butter sizzles and foams, add the sage and cook until the butter just starts to turn golden brown. Remove the sauce from heat, and add the walnuts and a little salt and pepper.

In a large pot of boiling water, cook the tortelli al dente, drain them, and transfer them to a warmed serving bowl. Pour the sauce over the tortelli, toss gently, and serve immediately.

EGG PASTA

This recipe makes enough pasta for 4 main-course servings, or 6 to 8 first-course servings of filled pasta.

2 cups (475 ml) unbleached flour
2 extra-large eggs

Heap the flour in a bowl and make a well in it. Break the eggs into the well and beat them together with a fork. Stir them into the flour from the bottom of the well until the dough in the center is smooth and shiny. With your hands, incorporate the flour from the outside into the center, kneading gently until the mass of dough is uniform in consistency but still soft. It should be smooth and resilient. You may not be able to incorporate all of the flour. Conversely, if the dough is sticky or very pliable, knead more flour into it. Divide the dough into two portions and cover it with plastic wrap or an overturned bowl. Let it rest for at least 15 minutes before putting it through a pasta machine.

To mix the dough in a food processor, put the flour in the work bowl with the steel blade and pulse. Add the eggs and process about 30 seconds. The dough should just turn over itself at the top of the bowl. Stop the machine and pinch a bit of the dough together. If it coheres readily, turn it out onto a board and knead it. If not, add water, a teaspoonful (5 ml) at a time, and process. Be careful not to add too much water.

Processor dough is stiffer than hand-worked dough. Cover it and let it rest for at least 30 minutes before rolling.

Adjust the rollers of the pasta machine to their widest setting. Roll one portion of the dough through the machine. Fold it and run it through the widest setting another time or two. Always put an open side into the machine when adding folded dough. If the dough feels wet or sticky, dust it lightly with flour before running it through the machine.

Advance the rollers and put the dough through the machine without folding. Continue rolling the dough once through each setting without folding. The ideal thickness for filled pastas, cannelloni, fettuccine, or lasagne is a little less than a millimeter; this is the last setting on some machines, the next to the last on others. The pasta will be difficult to handle if it is rolled too thin.

When the pasta has been rolled to the correct thickness, cut the pasta into 12-inch (24-cm) lengths, reserving the odd-shaped pieces for another use. Lay the pieces of cut pasta on a smooth, lightly floured surface so that they do not touch. Roll out the other portion of dough. The pasta is ready to fill.

BUCKWHEAT NOODLES WITH CHARD, POTATOES, AND FONTINA CHEESE

When the weather is really cold, we like to prepare this hearty, peasant-style dish called pizzocheri in its original home of Lombardy, Italy. If you have time for a real treat, make homemade buckwheat noodles, following the pasta recipe on page 71 but substituting 1/2 cup (120 ml) of buckwheat flour for 1/2 cup (120 ml) of unbleached flour. Roll the pasta about 1/16 inch (1.6 mm) thick and cut it in rectangular pieces about 1½ by 3 inches (4 by 8 cm). Japanese soba noodles, made of buckwheat, are also good; they give the dish a different texture as they are almost as fine as angel hair pasta. This dish is best assembled just before serving, but the vegetables may be prepared ahead.

SERVES 6
About 1 pound (450 g) red-skinned potatoes, halved lengthwise
and cut into 1/4-inch (5-mm) slices
1 pound (450 g) chard
4 tablespoons (60 ml) extra-virgin olive oil
3 tablespoons (45 ml) unsalted butter
1 medium onion, chopped coarse
4 large garlic cloves, minced
Salt and freshly ground pepper
1 package soba noodles, 12 to 15 ounces (340 to 425 g), or 1 recipe buckwheat pasta
(see note above)
4 ounces (115 g) Italian fontina cheese, grated
Extra-virgin olive oil
About 2/3 cup (160 ml) freshly grated parmesan cheese

Parboil the potato slices until just barely al dente. Drain and refresh under cold water. Drain and reserve.

Add 6 to 8 quarts (6 to 8 liters) of water to a large pot and bring it to a boil.

Meanwhile, cut the chard leaves from the stems. Chop the stems into 1/2-inch (1-cm) pieces and chop or tear the leaves into large pieces.

In a large, noncorrodible sauté pan, heat the olive oil and butter over medium heat. Add the onion and stir for 1 minute. Add the chard stems and cook for about 4 minutes, stirring occasionally. Add the garlic, potato slices, and salt and pepper, and cook for 1 minute, stirring well. Add the chard leaves, cover, and cook over medium-low heat for 4 to 5 minutes. Stir well and taste for seasoning.

Salt the boiling water and add the pasta, stirring well during the first few minutes of cooking. Cook it al dente.

Drain the pasta and transfer it to the skillet. Sprinkle the fontina cheese over the pasta, drizzle on a little olive oil, add about 1/2 cup (120 ml) of the parmesan cheese, and toss well. Sprinkle the remaining parmesan over the top and serve in warm pasta bowls or transfer to a large, warm serving dish, garnish with the remaining parmesan, and place in a 300°F (150°C) oven for as long as 10 minutes before serving.

Sauces

SPINACH SORREL SAUCE

Some version of this sauce has been served with fish for centuries in Europe, especially in France, where sorrel is a favorite. We find this particularly good with well-flavored fish such as salmon (the color contrast is pretty, too), cod, and sea bass; it is excellent in small quantities with delicate fish such as sole. It is wonderful also with boiled or steamed potatoes and cauliflower. To remove the central stems from greens, fold the shiny side of each leaf inward and hold the leaf near its base in one hand. Take the stem in the other hand and pull it toward the point of the leaf.

MAKES ABOUT 2 CUPS (475 ML)
8 ounces (225 g) spinach, central stems removed
6 ounces (170 g) sorrel, central stems removed
1 large shallot, diced fine
3 tablespoons (45 ml) butter
1/2 cup (120 ml) whipping cream (double cream)
Salt and freshly ground pepper

Wash the spinach and sorrel well and drain them in a colander.

Soften the shallot in the butter in a large noncorrodible pan over medium heat. Shake the spinach and sorrel by the handful to remove excess water. Place each handful in the pan and stir well. Cover and wilt over medium heat, stirring occasionally.

When the leaves are completely wilted, about 5 minutes, stir in the whipping cream. Simmer, uncovered about 15 minutes, or until the leaves are very soft and have formed a sauce with the cream. Season with salt and pepper and serve hot.

WATERCRESS SAUCE

This tangy, peppery sauce is excellent with a variety of poached or steamed vegetables—artichokes, asparagus, beets, carrots, new potatoes—as well as hard-cooked eggs and poached or sautéed fish or chicken. For a simple spring meal, we make a platter of several of these and add some radishes, chives or green onions, and pumpernickel bread to serve with the sauce. When we are serving more than four, we make a double batch of sauce so there's no need for polite portions. Any leftover sauce, tightly covered, keeps well in the refrigerator for several days.

MAKES ABOUT 2 CUPS (475 ML)
2 bunches watercress, about 12 ounces (340 g)
2 large shallots, about 4 ounces (115 g), diced fine
1/2 cup (120 ml) extra-virgin olive oil
1 tablespoon (15 ml) lemon juice
1 to 2 tablespoons (15 to 30 ml) white wine vinegar
Salt and freshly ground pepper

Remove large stems from the watercress. Wash it well, shake or spin out the excess water, and place it in a food processor. Add the shallots, olive oil, lemon juice, and 1 tablespoon (15 ml) of the vinegar.

Pulse the mixture, stopping to scrape the sides of the bowl once or twice. The sauce should be medium smooth with some bits of watercress and shallot. Season with salt and pepper and additional vinegar if desired.

ARUGULA MAYONNAISE

The zingy, slightly bitter bite of arugula in this nontraditional green mayonnaise is delicious with artichokes, potatoes, slices of summer-ripe tomatoes, and grilled fish. It is also good in a salad tossed with pasta or roast chicken.

MAKES A GENEROUS 3/4 CUP (180 ML)
1 cup (240 ml) lightly packed arugula leaves, stems removed
1 garlic clove
1 extra-large egg yolk
About 1/2 cup (120 ml) extra-virgin olive oil
1 to 2 tablespoons (15 to 30 ml) lemon juice
Salt and freshly ground pepper

In a blender or food processor, combine the arugula, garlic, egg yolk, about 1 teaspoon (5 ml) olive oil, 1 tablespoon (15 ml) lemon juice, and salt and pepper. Puree these ingredients. With the motor running, add the remaining oil in a fine stream; the mixture will thicken as it emulsifies. Taste for seasoning and add a little more lemon juice, salt, or pepper if desired. Refrigerate the mayonnaise until ready to use.

Garden Cress and Mustard Vinaigrette

Both broadleaf and curly cress taste good in this thick green salad dressing. We like it best with hearty vegetable and/or meat salads. It goes particularly well with potato, artichoke, beet, and summer or winter squash salads, enhances leftover roast beef or chicken, and is delicious with steamed, poached, or grilled fish or chicken.

MAKES ABOUT 1 CUP (240 ML)

2 cups (475 ml) loosely packed cress leaves and tender stems, washed and dried
3 tablespoons (45 ml) white wine vinegar
2 tablespoons (30 ml) Dijon-style mustard
2/3 cup (160 ml) olive oil
Salt and freshly ground pepper

Place the cress in a blender or food processor. Add the vinegar and mustard. Start the machine and add the oil in a thin stream to make an emulsion. Season with salt and pepper.

MAIN COURSES

LAMB WITH LAMB'S LETTUCE AND POTATOES

Because this lettuce was found in English fields where sheep grazed and left their rich manure (which the lettuce thrives on), it came to be called lamb's lettuce. It is also called corn salad, mâche in French, and veldsla (field salad) in Dutch. The sweetness and softness of roasted garlic complements the delicate flavor of the lettuce and is a traditional partner of lamb.

SERVES 6 TO 8

Leg of lamb, about 5 pounds (2.3 kg)
5 tablespoons (75 ml) olive oil
3 pounds (1.4 kg) russet potatoes
Salt and freshly ground pepper
6 to 8 fresh thyme sprigs, or 1 teaspoon (5 ml) dried thyme
1 head garlic, roasted
4 tablespoons (60 ml) sherry vinegar
3 tablespoons (45 ml) extra-virgin olive oil
1½ tablespoons (22 ml) walnut or hazelnut oil
1½ to 2 quarts (1½ to 2 liters) lamb's lettuce, trimmed and cleaned

Bone the lamb or have your butcher do it, keeping the natural muscle separations intact as much as possible. Trim the lamb of all fat and connective tissue. You will have three or four large pieces, and three or four small pieces. Rub the lamb all over with about 1 tablespoon (15 ml) olive oil. Cover tightly with plastic wrap and keep at cool room temperature while you prepare the potatoes.

Preheat the oven to 400°F (200°C). Scrub the potatoes well, halve them lengthwise if they are large, and slice them about 1/4 inch (5 mm) thick. Line two large sheet pans with baking parchment. Spread the potato slices on the pans. Scatter or sprinkle the thyme over them. Drizzle each pan of potatoes with about 1 tablespoon (15 ml) of olive oil and season with salt and pepper. Toss them well and shake to distribute.

Bake the potatoes for 20 minutes, remove the pan from the oven and shake it to loosen the potatoes, and turn them with a spatula. Bake for 25 minutes longer. While the potatoes are baking, finish preparing the salad and lamb.

Squeeze the roasted garlic into a small bowl. Stir in the vinegar. Drizzle in the extra-virgin olive and walnut oils while stirring to make an emulsion. Salt and pepper the vinaigrette and add more the vinegar if necessary; the vinaigrette should taste quite sharp.

In a sauté pan large enough to hold the lamb, heat the remaining 2 tablespoons (30 ml) of olive oil over medium-high heat. Add the large pieces first; they will be medium-rare in about 20 minutes. Turn frequently to brown the lamb evenly. After 8 to 10 minutes, add the small pieces and turn frequently. Place the cooked lamb on a platter and season with salt and pepper. Remove any fat from the pan and deglaze the pan with 1/2 cup (120 ml) water; reduce it to 2 to 3 tablespoons (30 to 45 ml) and add to the vinaigrette. Let the lamb stand while you finish the potatoes and vinaigrette.

When the potatoes are tender and golden brown, place them on a serving platter. Drizzle about 3 tablespoons (45 ml) of the vinaigrette over them. Toss the lamb's lettuce with 3 to 4 tablespoons (45 to 60 ml) vinaigrette and place the lettuce on the potatoes.

Cut each piece of lamb into thin slices on a slight diagonal. Collect all the juices and stir them into the vinaigrette.

Arrange the lamb on top of the lettuce and drizzle with the remaining vinaigrette. Serve immediately.

Frittata with Greens

We use the term "frittata" a bit loosely here; the dish is prepared like a traditional frittata, but it is not totally egg-encased: the greens and bits of red pepper stick out all over the top, which we find rustically appealing. This is a delicious treatment of kale; you may turn professed kale haters into passionate converts. Kale takes a bit longer to cook than most greens, and market kale a minute or two longer than your garden-grown Red Russian or Dwarf Curly Blue. Following the same formula, we like to make frittata with mixed spring greens: dandelion or broccoli rabe (both of which should be blanched for a minute or two first) and some tender marjoram, mint, and Italian parsley leaves.

SERVES 4

*About 1/2 pound (225 ml) kale, washed, stems removed, and cut or torn
into large bite-sized pieces
2 garlic cloves, minced
1 1/2 teaspoons (8 ml) olive oil
Salt and freshly ground pepper
1 tablespoon (15 ml) unsalted butter
Generous 1/2 cup (120 ml) chopped onion
1 small red bell pepper, roasted, peeled, stemmed, seeded, and cut into 1/2-inch (1-cm) dice
8 extra-large eggs, at room temperature, beaten with 1 tablespoon (15 ml) water
1/2 cup (120 ml) freshly grated parmesan cheese*

Wilt the kale with the water that clings to it in a noncorrodible pot tightly covered, over moderate heat for about 5 minutes. It should be bright green but still a little tough. Add the garlic, stir, and cook 2 minutes longer. Add the olive oil and season with salt and pepper. Stir well, cover, and cook for another 2 minutes, or until the kale is done; it should be tender but chewy. Remove the pan from the heat. Preheat the broiler.

Melt the butter in a 12-inch sauté pan over moderate heat. Add the onion and sauté for about 4 minutes, stirring occasionally. Add the bell pepper and stir for another minute. Add the parmesan cheese to the eggs, season with salt and pepper, and blend well. Transfer the kale to the sauté pan, toss well with the onion and pepper and pour the egg and cheese mixture over all. With a spatula, spread the mixture quickly and evenly in the pan.

Cover the pan and cook over moderate heat for 4 to 5 minutes. With a spatula, gently loosen the frittata from the sides of the pan. Slide the spatula under the frittata to see if it is browning on the bottom. When the bottom is cooked, place the pan under the preheated broiler for about 2 minutes. The eggs should just be set on top; do not overcook. Remove the pan from the broiler, slide the frittata onto a large round platter and cut it into eight wedges. Serve hot, warm, or at room temperature.

CABBAGE ROLLS WITH LENTILS AND SPINACH

Unlike ordinary cabbage rolls, those filled with rice and ground beef and smothered in tomato sauce, these have a Southwestern flavor and are garnished with a mayonnaise sauce. They may be made ahead, refrigerated, and baked 40 to 45 minutes before you plan to serve them. Chipotles en adobo are smoked-dried jalapeños in tomato sauce sold in cans at Latin American markets and specialty stores. You may substitute about 3 cups (710 ml) leftover black beans for the lentils.

MAKES ABOUT 12 CABBAGE ROLLS;
SERVES 12 AS AN APPETIZER OR 6 AS A MAIN COURSE
1¹/₂ to 2 pounds (675 to 900 g) cabbage
Salt and freshly ground pepper
About 1 tablespoon (15 ml) olive oil
3/4 to 1 teaspoon (4 to 5 ml) Hungarian paprika
1/2 pound (225 g) lentils, cooked until tender
1 roasted red bell pepper, peeled, stemmed, seeded, and diced
1 medium onion, diced
3 garlic cloves, minced

1 teaspoon (5 ml) cumin seed, toasted and ground
About 1 pound (450 g) spinach, wilted and chopped, or 1 package frozen spinach,
thawed and drained
1½ to 2 cups (360 to 475 ml) grated monterey jack cheese with jalapeños
1 extra-large egg yolk
1 tablespoon (15 ml) lemon juice
Pinch of sugar
1 chipotle en adobo
1/4 cup (60 ml) canola or vegetable oil
About 1/4 cup (60 ml) olive oil

Oil a 13 × 9 × 2-inch baking dish. Place about 6 cups (1½ liters) of water in a large non-corrodible pot and bring it to a boil. Remove twelve to fifteen outer leaves of the cabbage. Reserve. Slice the remaining cabbage about 3/8 inch (8 mm) thick and cut the slices into pieces 1 to 1½ inches (2 to 4 cm) long. Lightly salt the water and blanch the reserved outer cabbage leaves in the pot for about 2 minutes, or until they are just tender. Remove the leaves, drain, and let them cool.

Return the water to a boil and blanch the chopped cabbage for about 2 minutes, or until it is wilted, but still crunchy. Drain the cabbage and spread it in the prepared baking dish. Season the cabbage with salt, pepper, and about 1/2 teaspoon (2 ml) paprika. Drizzle on about 2 teaspoons (10 ml) olive oil and toss lightly. Preheat the oven to 350°F (180°C).

Combine the cooked lentils with the bell pepper, onion, garlic, cumin, spinach, and cheese. Season the mixture with salt and pepper and mix thoroughly. Place about 1/2 cup (120 ml) of the mixture on each of the cabbage leaves, fold in the thicker core end, then the sides, and roll up the leaves. Place the cabbage rolls on the chopped cabbage. Brush the rolls with the remaining teaspoon of oil and dust them lightly with the remaining paprika. Bake the rolls and chopped cabbage in a preheated oven for 30 to 40 minutes, or until the rolls are cooked through and bubbling.

While the rolls are baking, prepare the mayonnaise. Combine the egg yolk, lemon juice, sugar, salt, and chipotle in a blender and blend until smooth. With the motor running, add the vegetable or canola oil, then the olive oil in a fine stream until the mayonnaise has emulsified. Taste for seasoning and add a little more lemon juice, salt, or pepper if desired. Refrigerate the mayonnaise until ready to use.

Serve the cabbage rolls with some of the chopped cabbage and garnish them with the mayonnaise, or pass the mayonnaise on the side.

The inspiration for this dish is Southern Maryland Stuffed Ham from our *Chesapeake Cookbook*. Here, different greens create different flavors. For a sharp, defined flavor that plays well against the ham, use mustard greens or field cress. For a hearty flavor, use kale and/or chard. For a mild vegetable flavor, use watercress and/or collards. The ham and greens are tasty at room temperature and great in sandwiches.

SERVES 6 TO 8

1 spiral-sliced ham, about 6 to 7 pounds (2.7 to 3.2 kg)
12 ounces (340 g) kale, mustard greens, field or watercress
1 pound (450 g) collards or chard
1 pound (450 g) cabbage
1 medium onion, diced fine
3 to 4 large garlic cloves, chopped
1 tablespoon (15 ml) olive oil
1 bunch green onions, sliced thin with some green
1 tablespoon (15 ml) mustard seed
1 teaspoon (5 ml) cayenne pepper, optional
1 teaspoon (5 ml) freshly ground black pepper
1 teaspoon (5 ml) salt
1/2 cup (120 ml) apricot jam or preserves

Place the ham on a piece of heavy duty aluminum foil 3 to 4 feet (90 to 120 cm) long in a baking dish.

Trim the greens of large stems. Cut kale, mustard greens, collards, or chard into 1/2-inch (1-cm) shreds. Blanch kale or collards for 5 minutes, chard or mustard greens for 2 minutes. Steam field cress or watercress until the leaves just wilt and turn bright green, about 30 seconds. Refresh the greens under cold water and drain.

Remove any tough or limp outer leaves from the cabbage, core it, and cut it into 1/2-inch (1-cm) shreds; blanch them 5 minutes. Refresh the cabbage under cold water and drain.

If you used field or watercress, chop it coarse. Press the greens and cabbage well to remove excess water, but do not squeeze. Place the vegetables in a large bowl.

Soften the onion and garlic in the olive oil in a sauté pan over medium-low heat and add them to the bowl of greens. Add the green onions, mustard seed, cayenne pepper, black pepper, and salt. Mix well.

Stuff the greens mixture loosely between the slices of ham. Wrap the ham tightly in the foil. You may refrigerate it at this point for as long as 24 hours. Remove it from refrigerator an hour before baking.

Preheat the oven to 350°F (180°C). Bake the ham for 1 hour.

Place the apricot jam in a small saucepan and thin it with 2 tablespoons (30 ml) water. Heat the jam until it is just fluid.

Remove the ham from the oven. Fold the foil back and spread the top of the ham with the jam. Return the ham to the oven and bake it, uncovered, for 15 minutes longer. Remove it from the oven and let it stand for 10 minutes or so.

Lift the ham from the foil and place it on a serving platter. Finish slicing the ham and serve hot. If serving at room temperature, let it cool completely before removing the foil, slicing, and arranging the slices on a platter.

TURKEY WITH CURRIED GREENS

This dish is mildly Indian in flavor because of the curry powder, but you could leave the curry out if it doesn't appeal to you. The flavor of the greens is softened by goat cheese. To accentuate the Indian style, serve the dish with a simple mint chutney made of pureed mint leaves and green garlic (or green onions and garlic cloves) with a pinch of cayenne and plenty of plain rice or rice pilaf to soak up the delicious juices.

SERVES 6 TO 8

2 pounds (900 g) turkey breast cutlets
4 garlic cloves
2 teaspoons (10 ml) cumin seed, toasted and ground
1/8 teaspoon (0.5 ml) cayenne pepper
4 tablespoons (60 ml) olive oil
Salt and freshly ground pepper
3/4 pound (340 g) strong-flavored greens such as mustard, broccoli rabe, or turnip greens
3/4 pound (340 g) mild greens such as spinach, chard, or beet greens
1 medium onion, diced fine
2 tablespoons (30 ml) mild curry powder
1 tablespoon (15 ml) grated fresh ginger
6 ounces (170 g) mild fresh goat cheese

Pound the turkey cutlets about 1/4 inch (5 mm) thick. Crush the garlic cloves into a small dish and mix them with the cumin, cayenne, and 1 tablespoon (15 ml) olive oil. Season well with salt and pepper. Spread the paste on both sides of the cutlets, cover, and let stand at room temperature while you prepare the greens.

Trim the strong-flavored greens of large stems, wash them well, and blanch them for 2 minutes. Refresh them under cold water and drain. Trim the mild greens of large stems and wash them well.

Cut all the greens in about 1/2-inch (1-cm) shreds.

Heat 3 tablespoons (45 ml) olive oil in a large sauté pan over medium heat. Add the onion and sprinkle it with the curry powder. Add the ginger and cook about 5 minutes, or until the onion is soft.

Add the mild greens to the pan, cover, and wilt them, stirring occasionally, for about 3 minutes. Add the blanched greens to the pan and cook 2 minutes longer. Adjust the seasoning with salt, pepper, and more curry powder if desired. Transfer the mixture to a bowl to cool.

Preheat the oven to 400°F (200°C). Stir the goat cheese into the greens mixture. Lightly oil a baking dish large enough to hold half the cutlets in one layer. Cover the bottom of the dish with a thin layer of greens. Arrange half of the cutlets on top. Cover with half of the remaining greens. Make another layer of turkey and greens.

Bake for 15 minutes, then reduce heat to 350°F (180°C). Bake 15 minutes longer, or until the turkey is done and the greens are bubbling. Serve hot.

COD WITH LEEKS AND SPINACH

When we first returned from Italy in 1978, we made this dish frequently with either spinach or chard and salt cod, the flavor of which is particularly satisfying with these greens. Since then, salt cod has become a pricy gourmet delicacy rather than the peasant staple it was for centuries. If you try the recipe with salt cod, the amounts and procedures are the same. However, you will need to buy baccalà or boneless, skinless salt cod and soak it for 24 hours in three changes of water before making the dish. Whether you use fresh or salt cod, the dish has lots of lovely juices to serve with toasted country bread or mashed potatoes.

2 pounds (900 g) leeks, about 1 inch (2 cm) in diameter
1 tablespoon (15 ml) unsalted butter
1 tablespoon (15 ml) olive oil
1 medium onion, diced
2 garlic cloves, chopped fine
Salt and freshly ground pepper
2 pounds (900 g) spinach
2 pounds (900 g) fillet of cod or other flaky-fleshed white fish such as
halibut, scrod, or rock cod
1 cup (240 ml) heavy cream (double cream) or crème fraîche

Trim leeks of roots and tough outer layers, leaving 3 to 4 inches (8 to 10 cm) of tender pale green. Wash well and quarter lengthwise. Preheat the oven to 450°F (230°C).

Place the butter and oil in a sauté pan over medium heat. Add the onion and garlic and place the leeks on top. Cook the vegetables, covered, about 10 minutes, or until they release their juices and soften. Lower the heat if necessary to keep the vegetables from browning. Season with salt and pepper. Transfer the leeks to a plate and the onions and garlic to an ovenproof serving/baking dish large enough to hold the fish in one layer.

While the leeks, onions, and garlic are cooking, trim the spinach of roots and tough stems, and wash well. Shake the excess water from the spinach and place it in a large noncorrodible pan.

Cut the fish fillets on a diagonal about 1/2 inch (1 cm) thick. Remove any bones. Season the fish with salt and pepper. Place the fish on the bed of onions and garlic in the baking dish. Cover the fish with the leeks. Drizzle the cream over the dish. Bake for 10 to 12 minutes, until the fish is opaque and flaky.

During the last few minutes of baking the fish, place the pan containing the spinach over high heat and cover. Cook the spinach, stirring frequently, 3 to 4 minutes, or until it is just wilted.

Remove the fish from the oven and place the wilted spinach in the center of the dish or around the edges. Serve hot.

VEGETABLES

DUTCH-STYLE POTATOES WITH
CURLY ENDIVE OR ESCAROLE

Carolyn learned to make this dish from her husband, who is Dutch, but her sister- and mother-in-law have provided this definitive version. Mashed potatoes with vegetables and meat is a traditional Dutch dish called stamppot. This combination with bacon and endive or escarole is stimpstamp, and it has many variations. Some cooks use milk or cream in place of, or in addition to, the potato water. Some use kale or cabbage rather than endive or escarole. You will need about a pound (450 g) of cabbage or kale for this recipe. Many cooks season with nutmeg as well as salt and pepper. Stamppots are usually served as a family main dish in Holland.

SERVES 4 TO 6

*1/2 pound (225 g) pancetta (Italian-style unsmoked bacon rolled with pepper),
sliced thin and diced
1/2 pound (225 g) bacon, diced
1 large onion, diced
4 pounds (1.8 kg) russet potatoes
About 3/4 pound (340 g) curly endive or escarole
1 cup (240 ml) reserved potato cooking water
Salt and freshly ground pepper*

Place the pancetta and bacon in a large sauté pan over medium heat. When they are translucent and have rendered about half of their fat, add the onion. Reduce the heat to low and cook about 15 minutes, or until the onion is nicely browned and the pancetta and bacon are crisp.

Meanwhile, peel the potatoes and cut them in large chunks. Place them in a large pot, barely cover with water, and add 1/2 teaspoon (2 ml) salt. Bring to a boil, reduce the heat, and simmer about 15 minutes, or until potatoes are tender.

Trim the curly endive or escarole, and wash well. Cut large leaves in half lengthwise and cut the greens in fine shreds.

When the potatoes are done, drain them, reserving about 1 cup (240 ml) of the cooking water. Return the potatoes to the pan and place it over low heat. Add the shredded greens by the handful and mash them into the potatoes with a potato masher. Add the reserved cooking water gradually as you mash; use as much water as you need for the consistency you like. The traditional consistency is rather firm. Stir in the pancetta, bacon, and onions. Season with salt and pepper and serve hot.

STIR FRY OF JADE AND RUBY GREENS

Most greens lend themselves to stir-frying. The following recipe brings the bright red of chard, the deep green of mizuna, and the pale green and white of leeks together for interesting colors, flavors, and textures. The tangy greens are accentuated by the vinegar and pickled ginger; you may substitute a tablespoon (15 ml) of freshly grated ginger for pickled ginger. If you substitute other greens for the ones given below, add fleshy greens, such as baby bok choi, when you cook the leeks. Stir-fried greens can accompany Oriental-style main courses or poached, sautéed, or grilled fish, chicken, or meat. Rice is almost obligatory.

SERVES 6

About 12 ounces (340 g) red chard, washed, with stems separated from the leaves
1 tablespoon plus 1 teaspoon (15 plus 5 ml) peanut, sesame, or other cooking oil
2 large leeks, trimmed, rinsed well, halved lengthwise, and sliced 1/4 inch (5 mm) thick
2 or 3 large garlic cloves, minced
1/2 pound (225 g) mizuna, dandelion, or small mustard leaves, washed and
cut into 1- to 1½-inch (2- to 4-cm) pieces
1/4 cup (60 ml) pickled ginger, chopped coarse
About 2 tablespoons (30 ml) soy sauce
2 tablespoons (30 ml) rice vinegar

Cut the chard stems into 3/4-inch (2-cm) pieces and tear or chop the leaves in large pieces. Heat the oil in a large skillet or wok over medium heat. Sauté the leeks, stirring, for 2 minutes. Add the chard stems and garlic, stir, and sauté for 2 minutes. Add the chard leaves, cover and cook for 2 minutes.

Add the mizuna and ginger; stir. Add the soy sauce and vinegar, toss well, cover, and cook for 1 to 2 minutes. Taste for seasoning; adjust with soy sauce, vinegar, or salt. Serve hot over rice.

GRILLED RADICCHIO AND ONIONS

Many greens are good grilled, but the ones that grow in heads, with cores, are best because they can be sliced or cut into wedges and will stay intact. Radicchio, escarole, and Belgian endive are all delicious candidates. The sweetness of the grilled onions contrasts with the bitterness of the radicchio or endive. The cooking time will depend on how hot your grill or broiler is and how far the vegetables are from the heat; take care not to let them burn.

SERVES 6

1 pound (450 g) radicchio or Belgian endive, quartered lengthwise if round, halved if conical
3 large Vidalia or other sweet onions, cut crosswise into slices 3/4 inch (2 cm) thick
About 1/2 cup (120 ml) olive oil flavored with 1 to 2 minced garlic cloves
Salt and freshly ground pepper

Preheat the broiler or prepare your grill.

To broil, adjust the broiler rack so that the vegetables will be 5 to 6 inches (13 to 15 cm) from the flame. Brush the vegetables with the oil and garlic and arrange them in a single layer on a lightly oiled broiler pan. Season with salt and pepper.

Broil the vegetables 4 to 8 minutes on each side, or until the radicchio or endive are golden brown on both sides and tender. If the vegetables are browning too fast, move them farther from the flame. The onions take longest to cook; they should be charred dark. Radicchio takes a little longer than endive, but they both cook more quickly than the onion.

To grill, brush the vegetables with the oil and garlic, season them with salt and pepper, and place them on a rack over a medium-hot grill, about 6 inches (13 to 15 cm) from the heat. Allow 8 to 10 minutes on each side for the onions and 4 to 6 minutes on each side for the radicchio or endive, or until it is golden brown and tender. Serve hot or warm.

JAMAICAN-STYLE GREENS

Susan discovered this method of preparing greens when she was in Jamaica, where allspice, the national spice, is used in many ways. Her cook prepared the dish with a Scotch bonnet pepper, and so it was very spicy; you may omit the chile or use a milder one. These greens are usually served with yams and jerk chicken or grilled fish.

SERVES 4 TO 6

2 pounds (900 g) spinach, chard, kale, collards, or a combination
2 tablespoons (30 ml) butter
2 tablespoons (30 ml) vegetable oil
1 small onion, diced fine
1/4 teaspoon (1 ml) freshly ground allspice, or to taste
Salt and freshly ground pepper
1 to 2 dashes Angostura bitters
1 small chile pepper, stemmed, seeded, and minced, optional

Stem and wash the greens. Put them in a noncorrodible pot with the water that clings to the leaves, cover, and cook over medium heat until wilted.

Heat the butter and oil in a sauté pan over medium heat and sauté the onion for about 5 minutes, stirring occasionally.

Roughly chop the wilted greens and add them to the onion along with the allspice, salt and pepper, bitters, and chile.

Stir well, cover, and cook the mixture over low heat for about 10 minutes. Adjust the seasoning and serve hot.

CHARD BAKED WITH PARMESAN CHEESE

Chard is much loved in Italy, particularly Tuscany, where this is a classic dish. Use white chard here; its thick, succulent stems make the dish especially tasty. For such a simple preparation, this dish has an excellent record of converting greens-haters into greens-lovers at our tables.

SERVES 6

3 pounds (1.4 kg) chard
Salt and freshly ground pepper
4 tablespoons (60 ml) unsalted butter
3/4 cup (180 ml) freshly grated parmesan cheese

Wash the chard well and cut off the stems. Trim the stems and cut them into 2-inch (5-cm) lengths. Cut the leaves crosswise into 2-inch (5-cm) strips.

Blanch the stems in lightly salted boiling water for about 3 minutes. Add the leaves and blanch for about 1½ minutes longer. Drain the chard well and transfer it to an oven-proof dish. Season lightly with salt and pepper.

Preheat the oven to 450°F (230°C). Brown the butter in a sauté pan. Pour the browned butter over the chard and toss well. Sprinkle the parmesan cheese over the chard. Bake 10 minutes or so, or until the parmesan is bubbling and pale golden brown. Serve hot.

Belgian Endive, Leek, and Golden Bell Pepper Gratin

The sweetness of roasted bell pepper and leeks complements the nutty bitterness of endive in this simple and flavorful gratin. It is particularly good with simple sautéed or roasted fish and chicken dishes, as well as with veal chops or scaloppine. It is also a good main course for lunch or a light dinner.

SERVES 4 TO 8

1 pound (450 g) Belgian endives, halved lengthwise and sliced
crosswise 3/8 inch (8 mm) thick
1 pound (450 g) leeks, washed well, halved lengthwise, and sliced
crosswise 1/4 inch (5 ml) thick
1 large or 2 small yellow bell peppers, roasted, peeled, seeded, and cut into pieces
about 3/8 by 1½ inches (0.8 by 4 cm)
1 to 1½ tablespoons (15 to 22 ml) olive oil
Salt and freshly ground pepper
2 tablespoons (30 ml) unsalted butter
1 garlic clove, pressed
2 tablespoons (30 ml) unbleached flour
1½ cups (360 ml) milk
4 to 5 dashes freshly grated nutmeg
3 to 4 dashes cayenne pepper
1/3 cup (80 ml) freshly grated parmesan cheese
1/2 cup (120 ml) coarse dry bread crumbs

Preheat the oven to 400°F (200°C). Lightly oil a 2½- to 3-quart (2.5- to 3-liter) gratin or baking dish. Toss the endive, leeks, and bell pepper together and place them in the gratin dish. Drizzle the remaining oil over them and season generously with salt and pepper. Bake for 10 minutes.

Meanwhile, prepare the sauce. Melt the butter in a saucepan over moderate heat, add the garlic, and stir 1 minute. Add the flour all at once and stir to combine. Continue cooking and stirring for 3 to 4 minutes. Pour in about 1/2 cup (120 ml) of the milk and whisk vigorously. Add the rest of the milk and whisk until the sauce is blended. Season the sauce with salt, pepper, nutmeg, and cayenne. Continue cooking for 5 to 7 minutes, stirring as the sauce thickens. Stir in the parmesan cheese and cook 2 to 3 minutes longer; do not allow the sauce to boil. Adjust the seasoning if necessary.

Remove the vegetables from the oven and stir them gently. Pour the sauce over them, mixing gently to combine. Sprinkle the bread crumbs on top and return the dish to the oven. Bake 20 to 25 minutes longer, or until the gratin is golden brown and bubbling. Serve hot.

Salads

BEET AND BEET GREEN SALAD

Roasted beets, which we first discovered when we lived in Italy twenty years ago, have a wonderfully intense flavor. Though quite simple, the salad is pretty, with dark red beets, bright red stems, and bright deep green leaves. Golden beets or Chioggia (red and gold or white concentric circles) are also good prepared this way. The salad may be prepared a few hours ahead, though the beets run a bit. Beets stain clothing and cutting boards. We peel and trim them directly over the compost bucket, and slice them in our hands or on a plate with a small knife.

SERVES 6

3 pounds (1.4 kg) beets, about 2 inches (5 cm) in diameter, with tender greens
Salt and freshly ground pepper
About 3 tablespoons (45 ml) extra-virgin olive oil
About 3 tablespoons (45 ml) red wine vinegar

Preheat the oven to 400°F (200°C). Cut the greens from the beets, leaving about 1 inch (2 cm) of stems on the beets. Trim the tails of the beets to about an inch (2 cm). Scrub the beets well.

Wrap each beet tightly with doubled aluminum foil. Place the beets in a baking dish and bake about 1 hour, or until tender. Remove the beets from the dish and cool until beets can be handled. Remove the foil. Trim and peel the beets while they are still warm. Slice the beets thinly and season with salt and pepper. Toss with a tablespoon (15 ml) each of olive oil and vinegar.

Meanwhile, prepare the beet greens. Cut the leaves from the stems. Cut the stems in two to three pieces. Rinse the leaves and stems well. Blanch the stems for about 4 minutes in boiling lightly salted water. Add the leaves and cook until just tender, another 2 or 3 minutes. Drain the greens well and cool until warm to the touch. Toss with the sliced beets and the remaining olive oil and vinegar. Adjust the seasoning and serve.

RADICCHIO AND FENNEL SALAD

Radicchio, fennel, and balsamic vinegar are a combination that we have eaten happily for years. Bitter, sweet, and tart are present in different intensities, making this a dish in which every bite is interesting. You may substitute mild lettuce for half of the radicchio and/or leave out the anchovies. Supermarket radicchio is a ball-headed Verona type, which is good, but the salad is especially beautiful and tasty when the pointed leaves of Treviso, and the variegated and ruffled leaves of Castelfranco are used as well.

SERVES 4 TO 6

2 small fennel bulbs, about 1 pound (450 g)
About 12 ounces (340 g) radicchio
4 anchovy fillets, preferably salt-pack
1 garlic clove
3 tablespoons (45 ml) extra-virgin olive oil
About 1 1/2 tablespoons (22 ml) balsamic vinegar
Salt and freshly ground pepper

Trim the fennel and reserve the stalks and leaves for another use. Slice the bulb lengthwise about 1/8 inch (3 mm) thick. Separate the pieces.

Trim, wash, and core the radicchio. Tear the leaves into large bite-sized pieces.

Mash the anchovies with the garlic to make a paste. Place it in a small saucepan with the olive oil and heat over low heat. Add the vinegar and heat through.

Toss the radicchio and fennel with the warm dressing and serve immediately.

FRISÉE, ORANGE, AND GREEN ONION SALAD

Frisée is the term used for small, blanched heads of curly endive grown especially for salad. Wonderfully refreshing and juicy, this simple salad is sweet, bitter, and tangy. It brightens any meal. During the summer, seeded Valencia oranges can substitute for navels.

SERVES 4 TO 6

1 large head frisée, washed, dried, and torn into pieces
2 large or 3 medium navel oranges, peeled, sectioned, and sliced crosswise into fourths
5 to 6 green onions, sliced
Scant 1/2 cup (120 ml) extra-virgin olive oil
1/4 cup (60 ml) fresh orange juice
1 garlic clove, pressed or minced
Salt and freshly ground pepper

Arrange the frisée on a serving platter. Scatter the oranges over the frisée and garnish with the green onions.

In a small bowl, combine the oil, orange juice, garlic, salt, and pepper. Blend well with a fork. Pour the dressing over the salad and serve immediately.

BABY LETTUCE AND MÂCHE SALAD WITH FLOWERS

The greens and flowers in this salad will vary according to what is in season; use whatever small-leaved greens and flowers appeal to you. In early spring, violas, pansies, and Johnny-jump-ups are available for the flower garnish; later, choose from broccoli rabe, mustard, bok choi, and rocket flowers. In early summer, nasturtiums, daylilies, coriander, and chervil flowers are good, and late summer brings an abundance of herb blooms, as well as Gem marigolds.

SERVES 6 TO 8

About 8 cups (2 liters) of salad greens (baby lettuces, chicory, endive, rocket,
watercress, or spinach)
At least 2 cups (475 ml) mâche leaves
About 1 cup (240 ml) of assorted edible flowers
About 1/2 cup (120 ml) extra-virgin olive oil
2 to 3 tablespoons (30 to 45 ml) balsamic, tarragon, or herb vinegar
Salt and freshly ground pepper

Wash the salad greens well and pat or spin them dry. If the leaves are large, tear them into large bite-sized pieces. Gently rinse the flowers and pat them dry.

In a small bowl, combine the oil and vinegar with a fork, and season with salt and pepper. Adjust the seasoning if necessary.

Arrange the greens on a serving platter and place the flowers decoratively on top. At the table, stir the vinaigrette well and drizzle about half of it over the salad. Toss gently, add more vinaigrette if necessary, and serve immediately.

ORIENTAL-FLAVOR CABBAGE SLAW

Slaws offer so many possibilities for different flavors that we are always glad to experiment with them and to eat the results. This one is good whenever you want the flavors of the Orient without stir-frying. It is a crunchy fresh accompaniment to take-out noodles or barbecue.

SERVES 6

3/4 pound (340 g) Napa cabbage
3/4 pound (340 g) red cabbage
2 large carrots, grated
4 to 5 green onions, trimmed with 4 inches (10 cm) of green, and sliced thin on a diagonal
1/4 cup (60 ml) rice vinegar
2 tablespoons (30 ml) soy sauce
2 tablespoons (30 ml) olive or salad oil
1 1/2 teaspoons (8 ml) dark sesame oil
1 1/2 tablespoons (22 ml) grated ginger
2 garlic cloves, crushed
1/2 star anise, ground, or 1/2 teaspoon (2 ml) ground star anise
Pinch of sugar
Pinch of red pepper flakes, optional
Salt
Handful of mizuna greens or tat soi, trimmed and cleaned, for garnish

Trim the Napa and red cabbages and shred them fine. Mix the cabbages with the carrots and green onions in a large serving dish.

Place the rice vinegar and soy sauce in a small bowl. Whisk in the oils, ginger, garlic, star anise, sugar, and optional red pepper flakes. Toss the slaw with the dressing and let it stand at cool room temperature for 30 minutes to an hour.

The slaw may be refrigerated, tightly covered, for as long as 24 hours, tossing it once or twice. Bring the slaw to cool room temperature, taste, and adjust the seasoning if necessary. Just before serving, garnish the slaw with mizuna greens or tat soi.

Buttercrunch Lettuce, Watercress, and Persimmons with Raspberry Vinaigrette

This fruity, slightly peppery autumn salad is colorful and rather elegant. It is good before or after roasted or grilled poultry or game birds, especially duck, quail, squab, and pheasant, and makes even roast chicken or Cornish game hen seem a little special. It is also a good choice to follow a full-flavored pasta main course, such as the Greens-Filled Tortelli, page 70. For a nuttier taste, substitute arugula for the watercress.

Serves 4

1 head Buttercrunch or Boston lettuce
1 bunch watercress
2 large or 4 small perfectly ripe persimmons
1½ tablespoons (22 ml) raspberry or black currant vinegar
2 tablespoons (30 ml) hazelnut oil
3 tablespoons (45 ml) extra-virgin olive oil
Salt and freshly ground pepper

Wash and spin-dry the lettuce leaves. Wash the cress, remove large stems, and spin-dry.

Peel the persimmons. Carefully slice large ones into eight pieces lengthwise, or quarter small ones lengthwise.

In a small bowl, combine the vinegar and oils with a fork. Season with salt and pepper, and add more vinegar if desired.

Arrange the greens on four salad plates. Lay the persimmon slices on the greens. Stir the vinaigrette and drizzle a few spoonfuls over each salad. Serve immediately. Garnish with a little freshly ground pepper, if desired.

In early spring when the ground is soft enough to weed dandelions, or when your market has tender ones, this salad makes good use of the greens. Serve it hot or let it cool to room temperature.

SERVES 6

1/2 pound (225 g) dandelion greens, picked over, washed, and dried
1¹/₂ pounds (675 g) red-skinned potatoes
1/3 cup (80 ml) extra-virgin olive oil
Zest from 1 lemon: about 1¹/₂ teaspoons (8 ml)
3 garlic cloves, pressed or minced
Salt and freshly ground pepper
Juice from 1 large lemon: about 1/4 cup (60 ml)
Generous 1/4 cup (60 ml) pitted and sliced Kalamata olives

Remove the dandelion leaves from the stems and tear or chop the leaves into large bite-sized pieces. Cut the stems into pieces about 3/4 inch (2 cm) long.

Scrub the potatoes. If they are less than 2 inches (5 cm) in diameter, slice them about 1/8 inch (3 mm) thick; halve larger ones lengthwise and then slice 1/8-inch (3 mm) thick. Place the potatoes in a pot, cover them with water, and salt lightly. Bring to a boil, cook 10 to 12 minutes, or until crisp-tender, drain, and cover to keep warm.

Mix the olive oil, lemon zest, and garlic in a small bowl with a fork. Season with salt and pepper and blend well. Place about 2 tablespoons (30 ml) of the oil mixture, including some bits of garlic, in a sauté pan. Heat over medium heat and add the dandelion stems. Cook and stir for 4 minutes. Add the greens and stir for a minute longer. Season with salt and pepper. The stems should be cooked but still crisp, and the greens should be barely wilted.

Transfer the dandelions to a bowl and cover with the hot potatoes. Add the lemon juice to the remaining oil mixture, stir well, and pour over the hot vegetables. Add the olives and toss well. Taste for seasoning and add more salt, pepper, oil, or lemon if necessary. Toss well before serving.

Mixed Lettuces with Pears, Fennel, Walnuts, and Parmesan

This is a special salad in the fall and winter when many greens, pears, walnuts, and fennel are in season. We like an assortment of greens—some lettuces, a few of the bitter chicories, and some dark leaves like spinach and watercress. Comice, Bosc, or red Bartlett pears all work well in this recipe; they should be completely ripe. This is one of those dishes in which you can gather pieces of each different ingredient together to get the perfect bite. Our guests always come back for seconds; the recipe can be halved. Make parmesan curls by drawing a vegetable peeler over a piece of parmesan cheese.

Serves 8

About 6 cups (1½ liters) lettuce leaves, washed and torn into large bite-sized pieces
About 2 cups (475 ml) curly endive, escarole, or radicchio leaves,
washed and torn into bite-sized pieces
About 2 cups (475 ml) spinach, watercress, or orach leaves,
washed and torn into bite-sized pieces
1 medium fennel bulb, trimmed and sliced thin lengthwise
1 large or 2 medium pears, peeled, cored, quartered lengthwise, and sliced thin crosswise
About 1/4 cup (60 ml) parmesan curls
Generous 1/4 cup (60 ml) lightly toasted walnuts, chopped coarse
About 2 tablespoons (30 ml) sherry or balsamic vinegar
About 1/3 cup (80 ml) extra-virgin olive oil
2 tablespoons (30 ml) walnut oil
Salt and freshly ground pepper

Toss the greens together and arrange them on a large serving platter. Scatter the fennel and pear slices, and the parmesan curls over the greens. Sprinkle the walnuts over the salad.

In a small bowl, combine the vinegar, oils, and salt and pepper. Stir well with a fork. Taste, add more salt, pepper, or vinegar if necessary. Drizzle the dressing over the salad, toss well, and serve immediately or present the salad and pass the vinaigrette as it is served.

DESSERTS

Green Cake with Pistachios and
White Chocolate Ganache

We've wanted to create a green cake since we saw a photograph of the stunning-looking Vert-Vert cake from *Monet's Table: The Cooking Journals of Claude Monet* several years ago; this book has given us the enjoyable opportunity to do so. For any spring occasion, particularly St. Patrick's Day, it is a dramatic dessert. Despite its striking green color, the cake doesn't have a green flavor. It satisfies and brings compliments from our sweets-loving families and friends. You may substitute cornstarch for potato starch flour; the starch contributes to making the cake very light. Ganache is easy to make; the secret is to have it well-chilled before whipping.

Serves 10 to 12

Cake
Generous 1 pound (450 g) spinach, trimmed of large stems and washed
1/4 cup (60 ml) water
4 large eggs, separated, at room temperature
1 teaspoon (5 ml) pure vanilla extract
1/2 cup (120 ml) sugar
1/4 teaspoon (1 ml) salt
1/2 cup (120 ml) cake flour
1/2 cup (120 ml) potato starch or cornstarch
1/4 cup (60 ml) confectioners' sugar

Place the spinach and the water in a large noncorrodible pan. Cook over high heat, stirring, until the spinach is just wilted and bright green, about 1 minute. Refresh it under cold water and drain well. Press the spinach lightly to remove most of the excess liquid and puree it in a food processor or blender, adding a little of the cooking liquid if necessary for pureeing; then press the puree through a fine sieve. Reserve for cake and ganache.

Combine the egg yolks, 1/4 cup (60 ml) of the spinach puree, and the vanilla extract in the bowl of an electric mixer. Add 1/2 cup (120 ml) sugar and beat on medium-high speed about 5 minutes, or until the mixture is fluffy and ribbons fall from the beater.

Meanwhile, combine the salt and flours and sift. Preheat the oven to 350°F (180°C). Lightly butter a cake pan or springform pan that is 9 inches (23 cm) in diameter and 3 inches (8 cm) deep. Line the bottom with baking parchment or aluminum foil and butter lightly.

Beat the egg whites until they hold soft peaks. Add the confectioners' sugar in two batches, beating well after each addition. Beat the meringue mixture until it holds stiff, shiny peaks.

Stir about one-quarter of the whites into the yolk mixture with a rubber spatula. Fold in the flour and the remaining whites alternately in three batches.

Pour the batter into the prepared pan and smooth the top. Bake the cake for 25 to 30 minutes, or until the sides begin to pull from the pan and the top springs back when pressed with a finger.

Remove the cake to a rack and let it stand 10 to 15 minutes. Loosen the sides of the cake from the pan with a metal spatula, or remove the springform sides. Invert the cake and remove it from the pan, leaving the parchment or foil on the cake.

Set the cake, parchment or foil side down, on a rack and let it cool to room temperature. Remove the parchment or foil. The cake may be served when cool, double-wrapped and refrigerated for a few days, or frozen for as long as a month.

GANACHE

1¾ cups (620 ml) whipping cream
3 tablespoons (45 ml) spinach puree
6 ounces (170 ml) white chocolate, chopped fine
1/2 cup (120 ml) unsalted, shelled pistachio nuts, lightly toasted and chopped medium-coarse

In a heavy-bottomed, noncorrodible saucepan, scald the cream with the spinach puree. Remove it from heat and let stand for 2 to 3 minutes then strain it into a bowl. Sprinkle the white chocolate over the hot cream, stirring it into the cream as it melts. When all the chocolate is melted and the mixture is glossy and smooth, lay a piece of plastic wrap on the surface of the ganache and refrigerate it until it is well chilled. This will take about 2 hours, but you may prepare the ganache up to this point as long as 24 hours ahead.

When you are prepared to assemble the cake, whip the cold ganache with a hand-held whisk or the whisk attachment on an electric mixer until stiff peaks just start to form, as you would for soft whipped cream. The ganache will be too soft if you don't whip it enough, but will separate if you whip it too much.

ASSEMBLING THE CAKE

Cut the cooled cake with a serrated knife into three thin, horizontal layers. Place the bottom layer on a platter and frost it with about one-quarter of the ganache. Sprinkle with about one-third of the pistachios.

Continue layering and frosting the cake, sprinkling the pistachios only on the two bottom layers. After you have frosted the top and sides, lightly press the remaining pistachios into the frosting on the sides where the cake meets the platter. Refrigerate the cake until ready to serve, at least an hour. Remove it from the refrigerator 15 to 20 minutes before serving. The cake is best on the day it is made, but it may be held overnight in the refrigerator.

PINK LEMONADE AND SORREL SORBET

Uncooked sorrel has an oddly pleasant sourness and tartness; just describing it starts our salivary glands working. Usually we combine it with contrasting ingredients such as mild lettuce, cantaloupe, fish or chicken, or cheese or cream. We had the idea of playing up the tart flavor while we were taking a lemonade break from gardening on a hot day. We liked it with pretty pink lemonade and find this sorbet refreshing after a spicy meal or as a snack; we hope you will, too.

MAKES 1 QUART (1 LITER)
6 large or 8 average-sized lemons; 1 generous cup (240 ml) of juice
4 cups (1 liter) boiling water
1 cup (240 ml) sugar
2 tablespoons (30 ml) grenadine
About 6 ounces (170 g) sorrel

Place the lemon juice in a large pitcher and pour in the boiling water. Add the sugar and stir well to dissolve it. Add the grenadine, stir, and let the lemonade cool to room temperature.

Remove the stems from the sorrel and chop the leaves very fine. You should have about 2/3 cup (160 ml). Stir the sorrel into the cooled lemonade.

To freeze the sorbet in an ice cream machine, pour the lemonade into the container and process according to manufacturer's directions.

Otherwise, pour the lemonade into a large stainless steel bowl, cover, and place it in the freezer. Freeze until the lemonade is frozen hard, stirring once or twice. Remove the bowl from the freezer 20 to 30 minutes before serving the sorbet. Allow it to stand at room temperature for 10 to 15 minutes, depending on how hard the sorbet is and how hot your kitchen is.

Break the sorbet into chunks with an ice pick and place them in the container of a food processor. Process, stopping to scrape down the sides as necessary, until the mixture is smooth, but still frozen. Scoop into individual dessert dishes and serve immediately, or hold in the freezer for as long as 30 minutes.

SOURCES

Burpee and Company, W. Atlee
Warminster, PA 18974
(800) 888-1447

Cook's Garden
P.O. Box 535
Londonderry, VT 05148
(802) 824-3400

Hudson, J.L., Seedsman
P.O. Box 1058
Redwood City, CA 94064

Johnny's Selected Seeds
Foss Hill Road
Albion, ME 04910-9731
(207) 437-4301

Native Seeds/SEARCH
2509 N. Campbell Avenue #325
Tucson, AR 85719

Nichols Garden Nursery
1190 North Pacific Highway
Albany, OR 97321-4598
(503) 928-9280

Park Seed
Cokesbury Road
Greenwood, SC 29647-0001
800-845-3369

Pinetree Garden Seeds
Box 300
New Gloucester, ME 04260
207-926-3400

Seeds of Change
P.O. Box 15700
Santa Fe, NM 87506-5700
(505) 438-8080

Shepherd's Garden Seeds
30 Irene Street
Torrington, CT 06790
(203) 482-3638

Territorial Seed Company
P.O. Box 157
Cottage Grove, OR 97424
(503) 942-9547

BIBLIOGRAPHY

Books

Creasy, Rosalind. *Cooking From the Garden.* San Francisco: Sierra Club Books, 1988.

Dahlen, Martha, and Phillips, Karen. *A Popular Guide to Chinese Vegetables.* New York: Crown Publishers, 1983.

Dille, Carolyn, and Belsinger, Susan. *Herbs in the Kitchen.* Loveland, Colorado: Interweave Press, 1992.

Forsyth, Turid, and Mohr, Merilyn Simonds. *The Harrowsmith Salad Garden.* Ontario, Canada: Camden House Publishing, 1992.

Giacosa, Ilaria Gozzini. *A Taste of Ancient Rome.* Translated by Anna Herklotz. London: University of Chicago Press, Ltd., 1992.

Gilbertie, Sal. *Home Gardening at Its Best.* New York: Atheneum, 1977.

Harrington, Geri. *Grow Your Own Chinese Vegetables.* New York: Macmillan, 1978.

———. *The Salad Book.* New York: Atheneum, 1977.

Jabs, Carolyn. *The Heirloom Gardener.* San Francisco: Sierra Club Books, 1984.

Kasper, Lynne Rossetto. *The Splendid Table.* New York: William Morrow, 1992.

Larkom, Joy. *Oriental Vegetables.* Tokyo: Kodansha International, 1991.

———. *The Salad Garden.* New York: Viking Press, 1984.

Nash, Ogden. *Ogden Nash's Food.* Edited by Roy Finamore. New York: Stewart, Taboori, and Chang, 1989.

Phillips, Roger, and Rix, Martyn. *The Random House Book of Vegetables.* New York: Random House, 1993.

Proulx, E. Annie. *The Fine Art of Salad Gardening.* Emmaus, Pennsylvania: Rodale Press, 1985.

Reader's Digest. *Farmhouse Cookery.* London: Reader's Digest Association, 1980.

Root, Waverly. *Food.* New York: Simon and Schuster, 1980.

Tannahill, Reay. *Food in History.* New York: Stein and Day, 1973.

Taylor, Norman. *Taylor's Guide to Vegetables and Herbs.* Revised and edited by Gordon P. DeWolf, Jr. Boston: Houghton Mifflin, 1987.

Toussaint-Samat, Maguelonne. *A History of Food.* Translated by Anthea Bell. Cambridge, Massachusetts: Blackwell Publishers, 1992.

Periodicals

Bittman, Mark. "Leafy green and yellow bodyguards." *The New York Times Magazine,* April 25, 1993, p. 66.

DeBaggio, Thomas. *T. DeBaggio Plant Catalog and Garden Guide,* 1985 through 1994, Arlington, Virginia.

Gutfield, Greg, Maureen Sangiorgio, and Linda Rao. "Green eyes: can fruits and vegetables prevent cataracts?" *Prevention,* August, 1991, p. 10.

"Avoiding breast cancer through food choices." *Tufts University Diet & Nutrition Letter,* September, 1993, p. 1.

INDEX

RECIPES

BROCCOLI RABE
Penne with Broccoli Rabe, Pine Nuts, and Currants 69
Turkey with Curried Greens 85

BUTTERCRUNCH LETTUCE
Buttercrunch Lettuce, Watercress, and Persimmons with Raspberry Vinaigrette 102

CABBAGE
Baked Ham Stuffed with Greens 84
Cabbage Potato Caraway Soup with Croutons and Gouda 68
Cabbage Rolls with Lentils and Spinach 82
Naples-Style Cabbage and Endive Soup 65
Oriental-Flavor Cabbage Salad 101
Red Cabbage and Fontina Toasts 55

CHARD
Ancho Corn Pudding with Wilted Greens 58
Baked Ham Stuffed with Greens 84
Buckwheat Noodles with Chard, Potatoes, and Fontina Cheese 72
Chard Baked with Parmesan Cheese 93
Greens-Filled Tortelli with Sage Butter and Walnuts 70
Jamaican-Style Greens 92
Stir Fry of Jade and Ruby Greens 91
Turkey with Curried Greens 85

CHICORY
Baby Lettuce and Mâche Salad with Flowers 100

COLLARDS
Baked Ham Stuffed with Greens 84
Jamaican-Style Greens 92

CRESS
Baked Ham Stuffed with Greens 84
Fettuccine with Rocket, Cress, and Goat Cheese 67
Garden Cress and Mustard Vinaigrette 78
Watercress Sauce 76

DANDELION GREENS
Greens-Filled Tortelli with Sage Butter and Walnuts 70
Stir Fry of Jade and Ruby Greens 91
Warm Potato Salad with Wilted Dandelion Greens 103

ENDIVE
Baby Lettuce and Mâche Salad with Flowers 100
Belgian Endive, Leek, and

Golden Bell Pepper Gratin 94
Dutch-Style Potatoes with Curly Endive or Escarole 90
Mixed Lettuces with Pears, Fennel, Walnuts, and Parmesan 104
Naples-Style Cabbage and Endive Soup 65
see also Grilled Radicchio and Onions 91

EPAZOTE
Ancho Corn Pudding with Wilted Greens 58

ESCAROLE
Dutch-Style Potatoes with Curly Endive or Escarole 90
Mixed Lettuces with Pears, Fennel, Walnuts, and Parmesan 104
Naples-Style Cabbage and Endive Soup 65
Pizza with Escarole and Mozzarella 56
see also Grilled Radicchio and Onions 91

FRISÉE
Frisée, Orange, and Green Onion Salad 99

KALE
Baked Ham Stuffed with Greens 84
Black-Eyed Pea, Kale, and Turnip Soup 65
Frittata with Greens 81

LAMB'S LETTUCE
Lamb with Lamb's Lettuce and Potatoes 80

LAMB'S-QUARTERS
Ancho Corn Pudding with Wilted Greens 58

LETTUCE
Mixed Lettuces with Pears, Fennel, Walnuts, and Parmesan 104

MÂCHE
Baby Lettuce and Mâche Salad with Flowers 100

MIZUNA
Oriental-Flavor Cabbage Salad 101
Stir Fry of Jade and Ruby Greens 91

MUSTARD LEAVES
Ancho Corn Pudding with Wilted Greens 58
Baked Ham Stuffed with Greens 84
Stir Fry of Jade and Ruby Greens 91
Turkey with Curried Greens 85

ORACH
Mixed Lettuces with Pears, Fennel, Walnuts, and Parmesan 104

PERILLA
Sushi with Perilla 60

RADICCHIO
Grilled Radicchio and Onions 91
Mixed Lettuces with Pears, Fennel, Walnuts, and Parmesan 104
Radicchio and Bean Salad 61
Radicchio and Fennel Salad 98

ROCKET
Baby Lettuce and Mâche Salad with Flowers 100
Fettuccine with Rocket, Cress, and Goat Cheese 67

SORREL
Pink Lemonade and Sorrel Sorbet 108
Spinach Sorrel Sauce 76

SPINACH
Ancho Corn Pudding with Wilted Greens 58
Baby Lettuce and Mâche Salad with Flowers 100
Baked Spinach and Parmesan Gnocchi 54
Cabbage Rolls with Lentils and Spinach 82
Cod with Leeks and Spinach 86
Green Cake with Pistachios and White Chocolate Ganache 106
Jamaican-Style Greens 92
Mixed Lettuces with Pears, Fennel, Walnuts, and Parmesan 104
Spinach Sorrel Sauce 76
Turkey with Curried Greens 85

TAT SOI
Oriental-Flavor Cabbage Salad 101

TURNIP GREENS
Black-Eyed Pea, Kale, and Turnip Soup 65
Turkey with Curried Greens 85

WATERCRESS
Baby Lettuce and Mâche Salad with Flowers 100
Baked Ham Stuffed with Greens 84
Buttercrunch Lettuce, Watercress, and Persimmons with Raspberry Vinaigrette 102
Fettuccine with Rocket, Cress, and Goat Cheese 67
Mixed Lettuces with Pears, Fennel, Walnuts, and Parmesan 104
Watercress Sauce 76